The Fox, the Foetus and the Fatal Injection

To Jonathan, Tracy & family,
may Hashem bless you all
with health & happiness,
with best wishes,

Daniel

The Fox, the Foetus and the Fatal Injection

A thought-provoking Torah approach addressing the contemporary issues of abortion, assisted dying and euthanasia and their implications for the Jewish community

Rabbi Daniel Levy MA

Foreword by

Chief Rabbi Sir Jonathan Sacks

First published by Daniel Levy in Great Britain in December 2007.

To order more copies of this book or to contact the author please email: torahethics@gmail.com

A CIP catalogue for the record of this book is available from the British Library.

ISBN 978 0 9557825 0 3

Typeset in Minion Pro 11 pt.

Prepared and printed by:
York Publishing Services Ltd
64 Hallfield Road
Layerthorpe
York YO31 7ZQ
Tel: 01904 431213
Website: www.yps-publishing.co.uk

Contents

Gateshead Talmudical College

ישיבת
בית יוסף
גייטסהעד

Principal
Rabbi Z. Cohen

Rosh Hayeshiva
Rabbi A. Gurwicz

88 Windermere Street, Gateshead, Tyne & Wear NE8 1UB
Telephone: (0191) 477 2616 Fax: (0191) 490 0480

כ"ט ניסן תשס"ז

כבוד הרב דניאל לוי שליט"א
רבה של הקהילות המאוחדות בלידז

יורשה לי להביא ברכתי ברכת כהן לאדוני מותיקי תלמידינו לשעבר, כי שמעתי עליו עד כמה
שהוא פועל להרמת קרן הדת ומקדש שם שמים בפעולותיו הברוכות ובהנהגתו האישית,
כדוגמא איך צריך רב להתנהג עם קהל עדתו לרוממם ולהאיר דרכם ולקרבם לאביהם
שבשמים. ייסף ה' לו כח ואון לשמור משמרת הקודש, יעלה מעלה מעלה בתוי"ש לקדש שם
שמים וההצלחה תאיר לו פנים, והיות ועומד להוציא לאור עולם ספר על עקרי יהדות הנני בזה
לברכו כי ה' יצליח דרכו ויפוצו מעינותיו הברוכים חוצה

ואבוא בזה על החתום ובכבוד רב

זאב כהן
ר"מ ומנהל.

Hon Treasurer: I. Kaufman esq. Secretary: S. Esofsky esq.

Charity Commission No. 527414 Inland Revenue No. X576134

בית דין צדק דק"ק ליעדז והגליל
LEEDS BETH DIN
(JEWISH ECCLESIASTICAL COURT)
411 Harrogate Rd Leeds LS17 7BY
Tel. (0113) 269 6902 Fax. (0113) 237 0893

6 March 2007
ט"ז אדר תשס"ז

Dear Rabbi Levy,

I have browsed through your article on abortion and assisted death with great interest.

I found it well researched and presented, and reflects your scholarship and deeply held faith and the compassion that you show in your pastoral duties.

I greatly commend you for highlighting these crucial issues, the loss of life of perfect and innocent foetuses, particularly in Israel, and the dangers of assisted suicide.

I am sure that your work will be well received.

I wish you success in this and all your worthy endeavours.

Dayan Yehuda Refson.

February 21, 2007

Dear Rabbi Levy,

I was deeply impressed after reading your book, a book written in the language of truth. You are to be commended for raising topics which many would choose to ignore, and discussing them with clarity and conviction.

As you rightfully stated in your book, abortion is a plague of pandemic proportions. Modern medicine has made giant strides in prolonging life and curing disease, especially in children. Is it not ironic that the biggest killer of all remains unchecked?

EFRAT Organization has been dealing with the problem of abortion since 1977. Over the years we have saved tens of thousands of lives. After hearing thousands of stories, and dealing with women of all sorts, we have made an amazing discovery. *Never*, in all the years, have we encountered a woman who regretted maintaining her pregnancy. Once their babies were born, their mothers were thrilled with them, and rejoiced in them.

This fact is a very powerful one, and should be noted by professionals dealing with these issues. No other medical procedure, which a woman is considering, will enable her to say with perfect sincerity, "I have no regrets!"

The main cause of the spiraling abortion rates is simple ignorance. The women just don't know, are not aware that the child they are carrying is a viable human being from the first moments. Women, faced with social or economic pressure are very soon convinced that abortion is the solution.

Yes, indeed, biology is taught in schools worldwide, but emphasis is placed on frogs and butterflies, and the miracle of human development is neglected.

EFRAT is known today as Israel's largest lifesaving organization. We stand at the forefront of educating and raising awareness of the viable alternatives to murder. Your book is an important contribution to the success of our mission.

Sincerely,

Dr. Eli J. Schussheim
President
EFRAT

CHILDREN ARE OUR FUTURE

C.R.I.B.
Committee for the
Rescue of
Israel's   1612 57th St., Brooklyn,
Babies   N.Y. 11204-1832
            Tel. 1-800-273-4314

EFRAT
International
Organization   10 Harlev St. P.O Box 6125
for Saving   Jerusalem 91061 Israel
Jewish Babies   Tel. 972-2-653-6212   www.efrat.org.il
                 Fax 972-2-652-9531   efrat@efrat.org.il

Acknowledgements

"Rabbi Akivah said … More than the calf wishes to suckle the cow wishes to nurse."

(Talmud)[1]

From a young age I always wanted to be a rabbi and, indeed, with the help of the Almighty, I started work in my early twenties. That was some fifteen years ago, yet somehow it seems so close to me in time, that I had the privilege to study in Gateshead Yeshivah. The spirit of the Yeshivah and my teachers has stayed with me all these years. Over the years that I have been in the rabbinate I have found myself addressing certain key contemporary issues which I felt pricked my conscience and therefore I felt it necessary to share them with the congregation. It may sometimes seem to people, especially if they are not accustomed to rabbis speaking on contemporary issues, that there is an obsession with them. Indeed, I once found myself having to explain to someone that I was not obsessed with the subject of abortion, just simply felt it a necessary subject to talk about occasionally from the pulpit, especially when one considers that so many are silent on the matter. I have always felt passionately that Judaism must be seen as it really is. That is contemporaneous and up-to-date with something to say about almost every aspect of life. Much of this small book is a reflection on some of the topics I have addressed with members of the communities in which I have worked over the years. I have served first, Golders Green Synagogue, London where I had my first job as Youth Director and then Cardiff United Synagogue where I was Rav for six years and, most recently, the United Hebrew Congregation, Leeds where I have been the Rav for the last eight years.

I am grateful to the synagogues and organisations[2] which kindly gave me the opportunity to present a talk on the subject matter of this book. Much of the feedback was subsequently incorporated into later talks and is also included in this book.

I thank the Chief Rabbi, Sir Jonathan Sacks, for writing the foreword. It adds gravitas to this book and I am both honoured and humbled by this. The Chief Rabbi's own books have been a source of inspiration to me.

I have included two articles at the beginning of this book. The first highlights the issues concerning a doctor who has a conscientious objection to abortion and how this interfaces with their duty of care to their patients. This article is written by Dr James Gerrard and I am grateful to Sister Brigid Murphy from St. Gemma's Hospice, Leeds for introducing me to him. The second article by James Goss QC centres on Dr Moore who was accused of killing one of his patients. The purpose of this article is to illustrate the difficulties within the law of securing a conviction, even as the law stands at the moment, forbidding assisted dying and euthanasia. I am grateful to both contributors for the time they have taken to write these illuminating articles.

I must thank the various people who proofread and edited the work and who provided valuable suggestions. I particularly wish to thank Dayan Yehuda Refson, (Av Beth Din of Leeds), Rabbi Chaim Miller, Ronnie Cohen, Howard Jackson, Simon Jackson, Martin Glass and Freddy Apfel, who all painstakingly went through the entire book both editing it and making worthy suggestions. Dr Eli Schussheim the president of the Israeli (anti-abortionist) organisation Efrat who has given me great encouragement with his letter printed at the beginning of this book. Professor David Levene, who as well as proofreading the book, provided me with ancient classical literature on the secular view on autonomy. Dr John Sinson, who as well as proofreading the book, provided me with important relevant articles from the British Medical Journal and other worthy medical publications, saving me much time in my research. Elisabeth Baker who painstakingly undertook a final proofreading and remedied many grammatical and stylist errors. Above all, I would like to thank my dear wife Naomi who has always supported me and edited all my work. If something has been unclear she has helped me clarify my writing thereby making it understandable.

I conclude by giving thanks to the Almighty for having blessed me with a measure of courage to speak out on these issues of life and death and a modicum of wisdom to put pen to paper.

Daniel Levy
Leeds, United Kingdom 5768/2007

Notes

1. *T. B. Pesachim* 112a.

2. They are (listed in the order where I spoke), United Hebrew Congregation, Leeds; Jewish Doctors' Association, Leeds; Yeshurun Synagogue, Hale, South Manchester; Birmingham JSOC; Birmingham Jewish Education Board (BJEB) inter-communal adult education project and Edgware Adas, London.

Foreword
by Chief Rabbi Sir Jonathan Sacks

Two of the most transformative of all Biblical ideas are those of the dignity of the human person and the sanctity of human life. Both are stated near the beginning of the Hebrew Bible, the first in Genesis 1, the second in Genesis 9, and both are based on the axiom that, of all known life-forms in the universe, the human person is the only one to bear the 'image and likeness' of God Himself.

Just how radical this idea was and still is can be measured along many axes: from the appalling bloodshed of the twentieth century which witnessed the murder of more than a hundred million human beings at the hands of their fellow humans in the course of war, to the current massive figures of abortions performed throughout the West, to the increasing pressure on liberal democracies to permit voluntary euthanasia on the grounds of personal autonomy, that we should be free to do what we wish so long as there is no direct harm to others.

Without wishing to compare the gravity or scale of these phenomena, they are none the less stains on the conscience of humankind. Only the most serious threat to the health of the mother should lead us to terminate the life of an unborn child. Voluntary euthanasia is the start of a slippery slope toward involuntary euthanasia – murder by another name. The history of Germany in the 1930s and 1940s should be warning enough of where that may lead.

The word 'holy' means many things, but it includes

the idea that there are certain things that do not belong to us, chief of which is life itself. This is a religious idea, but it is one that can be explained in secular terms. There are things so important that they lie beyond the scope of human choice. They are non-negotiable, inalienable. Nowadays we use this idea in relation to human rights. But it applies also to human life. What it means is that there is a limit to autonomy. Not everything is determined by our choice. There are things that must be protected from human choice by law, if society is to be protected from our own worst instincts. Our contemporary society is one of the first in history to believe that there are no moral absolutes, and it is wrong so to believe. There are acts that are objectively forbidden, and taking innocent life, whether of the unborn child or the dying patient, falls within that moral prohibition.

Jewish law has clear teachings on these matters. But they are so grave that they form part of the Noahide covenant, Judaism's understanding of the universal moral principles that govern all humanity. In *The Fox, the Foetus and the Fatal Injection* Rabbi Daniel Levy has written a deeply felt and strongly argued work that deserves to be widely read and reflected on. It is a timely application of a timeless truth, that God is to be found in life, above all in human life, and that we cannot honour God by dishonouring the very life He has placed in our trust.

I commend this work highly. It is serious, germane and compelling. I would add one footnote. Ancient Greece saw nothing wrong with abortion. It permitted even infanticide. The story of Oedipus begins with his father Laius leaving him to die. Nor did the Greeks forbid euthanasia. The word itself, meaning 'an easy death', derives directly from the Greek.

Ancient Greece – Athens especially – was one of the greatest civilizations ever to appear on earth. Yet it lasted only briefly. Ancient Israel, by comparison, was a tiny people with little interest in, indeed principled disengagement from, the fields in which Greece excelled: painting, sculpture, architecture, drama, sport, philosophy and epic literature. Yet its civilization survives and thrives to this day.

What that story suggests is that cultures live or die by the moral principles they hold holy. Judaism taught that what matters to a civilization is not strength but its defence of the weak; not wealth but the help it gives to the poor; not power but its concern for the powerless. The counter-intuitive, yet profoundly moving lesson of history is that what makes a civilization invulnerable is the way it protects the vulnerable.

There are no more vulnerable people than the unborn child and the terminally ill patient. To hold their lives dispensable at the will of the parent or the patient is a temptation that we must resist. For when life ceases to be holy, something within a culture begins to die. The alternative, as imperative now as it was when first said 33 centuries ago, is Moses' great command: 'Choose Life.'

May Rabbi Levy's fine work help us to do just that.

Chief Rabbi Sir Jonathan Sacks
Ellul 5767/September 2007

Introduction

"Rabbi Tarfon said… the work is not for you to complete but neither are you free to desist from it."

(Mishnah)[1]

Abortion, assisted dying and euthanasia are some of the greatest moral, ethical and religious issues facing the Western world in recent times. Some 120,000 precious lives are aborted each day worldwide and more than 44 million are aborted annually.[2] The general rule of thumb of the Torah is that unless the foetus poses a serious threat to the life of the mother it may not be aborted. Governments of Denmark, the Netherlands, Belgium and the American State of Oregon all allow assisted dying and some of them even allow euthanasia, but that of course does not mean that other countries should simply follow suit. However, sadly, like a number of issues which governments have for a long time been reluctant to legalise, eventually they are legalised. Two examples are abortion (1967) and more recently same sex partnerships (2006). The case against assisted dying and euthanasia is clear according to the Torah way of thinking: murder is forbidden regardless of whether it is taking your life or someone else's. Each moment of life is sacred and it is not up to man to terminate actively life, despite the suffering and distress that one might endure.

It should be noted from the very outset that figures on the potential uptake of assisted dying and euthanasia in the

UK range from 650[3]–13,000[4] people a year. Predictably, those in favour of euthanasia project the 'lower' figure and those against project the higher figure.

Religious communities need not and should not be meek and go along with Western thinking if it goes against their religious beliefs. As a thinking religious community, we must contribute to and engage in the Torah way of thinking and alert fellow Jews and society as a whole to the enormity of these issues.

Chief Rabbi Sir Jonathan Sacks writes so aptly:

"We absorb moral ideas the way we learn a language, unconsciously; but there is much to be said, once in a while, for stepping back and asking why we came to see the world the way we did."[5]

This short book does not aim to revisit established issues in halachah regarding abortion and euthanasia. Numerous articles and books have been written about abortion and voluntary, involuntary, active and passive euthanasia. This particular contribution to the debate aims to achieve three things. First, to highlight the ethical distortion we have been faced with in recent decades with special reference to abortion. Secondly, to explore the issue of proposed assisted dying and euthanasia and religious and secular views on autonomy. Thirdly, to focus on the halachic ramifications for those who administer lethal injections, and deal with questions such as: what is their place in our community, are they to be shunned for transgressing halachah and whether they may be given honours in the synagogue? How do we view the person who agrees to undergo assisted dying or euthanasia? Is s/he to be regarded as a case of *wilful suicide* (a person of sound mind) or rather as an *un-wilful suicide* (a person of unsound mind)? I hope that for many this book will be iconoclastic, challenging the way a significant proportion of society currently thinks.

The subject is enormous and the task is daunting. I do not think that the views and opinions expressed here will curry favour with everyone and I do not think that everything I write will be as clear as I would like it to be, since the written word is always open to misinterpretation. But I am reminded of the adage from the great sage Rabbi Tarfon, "The work is not for you to complete but neither are you free to desist from it."[6] I will try my best and I hope that, with the help of the Almighty, I will make a small contribution to a valuable discussion on pertinent religious matters.

Daniel Levy
Leeds, United Kingdom 5768/2007

Notes

1. *Ethics of the Fathers* 2:21.

2. 54 countries allow abortion, which is about 61 percent of the world population. 97 countries, about 39 percent of the population, have abortion laws that make it illegal according to the pro-abortion Center for Reproductive Law and Policy in New York. The Alan Guttmacher Institute reports that approximately 22 million legal abortions were registered in 1987. It is estimated that between 4 and 9 million were not reported, totalling 26-31 million legal abortions in 1987 alone. There were a total of 10-22 million 'clandestine' abortions, bringing the total worldwide figure to 36 and 53 million abortions, www. abortionfacts.com/statistics/world_statistics.asp.

   In 2004 in Russia it was even more alarming, 1.5 million children born, yet 1.6 million children were aborted, *The Week,* 10 June 2006.

   It must be noted that both Rabbi Shlomoh Zalman Aurbach (*Shulchan Shlomoh,* volume 1, pp. 109-110) and Rabbi Moshe Feinstein (*Responsa Igrot Moshe* HM 2:73:8) forbid Jewish doctors from performing abortions on Gentile women as well.

3. M. A. Branthwaite, *Taking The Final Step: Changing The Law on Euthanasia and Physician Assisted Suicide,* BMJ, volume 331, 24 September 2005, p. 682.

4. R. J. D. George, I. G. Finlay and D. Jeffrey *Legalised Euthanasia Will Violate the Rights of Vulnerable Patients*, BMJ, volume 331, 24 September 2005, p. 684, with 2,000 occurring without request or consent.

5. Chief Rabbi Sir Jonathan Sacks, *To Heal a Fractured World*, (London: Continuum, 2005), p. 12.

6. *Ethics of the Fathers* 2:21.

Abortion from the Perspective of a General Practitioner with a Conscientious Objection

by Dr James Gerrard

Dr James Gerrard qualified from St. Andrews and Manchester UK in 1985. Since 1992 he has worked at the Windmill Medical Centre, Leeds. His interests within the practice include GP education and in particular being a mentor for the GP registrar.

This article illustrates how doctors' own moral perspectives interface with the duty of care for the patient.

For some people, the question of abortion is such that performing or undergoing the procedure would leave them untroubled by the smallest moral qualm. However, even in today's society, where abortion is perhaps the most commonly performed gynaecological operation, these individuals are in the minority. The rest of us hold a spectrum of opinion ranging from some who maintain an opposition under any circumstance, to those who profess a pragmatic acceptance of what they consider to be a necessary evil, but an evil none the less, and something that in a perfect world would not be necessary.

It is strange then, given that so many of us feel troubled by abortion, that so many are done, and that the numbers continue to rise. Doctors' opinions may mirror those of the community at large, but because many of us must deal with the issue in our daily work, our views are brought into sharper focus. Whether we are in favour of or against abortion, we should be prepared to explain our position, as our views have implications for other aspects of our working lives defined by a moral framework.

I am a GP in a busy city practice. I stand at the anti-abortion end of the spectrum of opinion on this subject, and express a conscientious objection to the current Abortion Act. Some might question that a doctor can take such a position without compromising the obligations due to his or her patients, or failing in the duty of care that is owed to them. I, however, argue to the contrary, and further, that it is quite possible for a doctor who is in *favour* of abortion to act in a way detrimental to the wellbeing of a patient who may come with a request for the operation.

As a family doctor I frequently encounter women faced with the dilemma of an unexpected or crisis pregnancy, and am witness to the distress which they may experience. For them the news of pregnancy can engender deeply mixed sensations. It may well be that they do not want to be pregnant. It might also be the case that they do not want an abortion either. Such competing emotions can be as unexpected as they are upsetting, and I feel that the failure by health care staff to allow these feelings to be adequately expressed and worked through is one of the key reasons why many women, having had an abortion, live to regret the decision.

Part of the problem is that as things stand, our default setting for a woman in a difficult situation is squarely in favour of abortion. Not only this, but because she is encouraged to view an abortion as her own "choice" (a strange notion, since many women opting for one do so because they feel they have no choice at all) any subsequent responsibility for the decision is thrust in her arms by the society which pressured her into making it. For the same reason there is little incentive for her to voice any objection to abortion afterwards; after all, she made her own decision in that direction, and we do not want her to suggest differently for anyone else. But is this fair? We do not advocate the legalisation of shoplifting as an answer for families with children to clothe and feed; we would seek a more just solution than that as a society. However, were a woman caught stealing bread to feed her hungry children, we would not expect her always thereafter to speak out in favour of theft.

When faced with a patient who requests an abortion, after discussing her circumstances and options with her, if she wishes to be referred for the procedure I inform her that I cannot do this for her, and that she will need to see another doctor in the practice for it to happen. This is in line with the guidance of both the General Medical Council and the British Medical Association. Of interest, the General Medical Council also has this to say:

"You must treat your patients with respect whatever their life choices and beliefs. You must not unfairly discriminate against them by allowing your personal views to affect adversely your professional relationship with them or the treatment you provide or arrange."[1]

This key phrase will often be taken to be directed at doctors with an anti-abortion viewpoint, and indeed it is. Less well recognised, I think, is the fact that of course this statement is highly relevant to those doctors who are in favour of abortion too, and that their views on the matter may unfairly influence a woman in conflict. That the balance of moral thinking may be skewed in this direction among the medical establishment is illustrated by an article, published in 2006 in the *British Medical Journal,* by Professor Julian Savulescu.[2] In *Conscientious Objection in Medicine* Savulescu argues the disturbing claim that "A doctor's conscience has little place in the delivery of modern medical care." For those of us who feel the opposite, that a conscientious sense of duty towards our work is imperative, this is a chilling viewpoint. For us, our clinical decisions have a moral dimension which impacts upon our patients' well-being. Savulescu's opinion that "Doctors who compromise the delivery of medical services to patients on conscience grounds must be punished" is shocking at least in part because one assumes it is those with the mind-set shared by the author who will be the judges.

If the tide of opinion on moral issues continues to run in the direction of Savulescu's article among medical policy makers, it may be that doctors with a conscientious objection will be marginalised or compromised in their ability to perform their work. That this would be detrimental to patient care seems obvious to me, and I would not be able to continue in my work as a doctor were this to be the case. I feel that there needs to be a sea-change in the way that doctors and society generally express their feelings on this important issue. Because current practice is set at a default biased towards abortion, the decisions of those for whom it presents no moral dilemma are favoured at the expense of the majority of women who remain troubled by the issue. It is vital that a way should be found to allow more of this larger group to keep their children. Conscientious objectors inside and outside of medical practice should continue to voice their concerns.

Notes

1. General Medical Council, *Good Medical Practice*, GMC, 13 November 2006.

2. J. Savulescu, *Conscientious Objection in Medicine*, BMJ, volume 332, 4 February 2006, pp. 294-297.

The Doctor and the Law of Murder
Regina v. Dr David Moor
by James Goss QC

Mr James Goss QC is both Head of Chambers at No. 6 Park Square, Leeds, and a member of 18 Red Lion Court, London. He practises almost exclusively in criminal cases – both prosecuting and defending – homicide, fraud, drug importation and health and safety cases. Amongst his most significant and notable cases are Dr David Moor (accused of killing his patient), Gary Hart (deemed responsible for causing the Selby Rail Crash), Nurse Julia Levitt (convicted of unlawfully killing her patient) and Peter Voisey (guilty of the kidnap and rape of a 5 year girl taken from her bath in Newcastle). Mr Goss is also a Recorder of the Crown Court.

This article shows how difficult it is to secure a conviction, even as the law stands now, prohibiting assisted dying and euthanasia.

Fifty years ago, in April 1957, Mr Justice Devlin directed the jury in the well known case of Dr Bodkin Adams,[1] a doctor being tried for the murder of a terminally ill patient, in the following terms:

"Murder is an act or series of acts ... which were intended to kill and did in fact kill the dead woman. It does not matter for this purpose that her death was inevitable and her days were numbered. If her life was cut short by weeks or months it is just as much murder as if it were cut short by years ... It remains the law that no doctor nor any man, no more in the case of a dying man than the healthy, has the right to deliberately cut the thread of life."

Morphine, either in its oral form or in the more potent from of diamorphine injected into a vein or under the skin (subcutaneously), is commonly prescribed for the relief of pain in terminal illness. One of its effects is to depress respiration, so care has to be taken to adjust the dose to a level which relieves pain without compromising respiration.

In July 1997 Dr David Moor, a Newcastle GP, boasted in interviews with a local journalist that he aggressively supported euthanasia and had administered lethal doses of diamorphine to two of his patients in the previous week. He repeated his claim in television and radio interviews. One of those patients was identified as George Liddell, an 85 year old patient suffering from bowel cancer who was bed-ridden, immobile and complaining of pain. One afternoon, whilst already in receipt of oral morphine, he let out a pronounced yell of agony on being moved; his daughter asked Dr Moor to seek his admission to a hospice and to take action to prevent him from suffering pain like that again. Dr Moor set up a syringe driver that automatically administered 30 mg of diamorphine subcutaneously every 6 hours for 24 hours. As a result, Mr Liddell fell into a deep, peaceful and pain free sleep. Nurses who attended all considered death was imminent: he looked and sounded extremely ill. The following morning, rather than cause the district nurse to refill the syringe driver, Dr Moor injected Mr Liddell with what he eventually claimed was a mixture of diamorphine and Largactyl, an anti-emetic prescribed to ease the 'retching' from which Mr Liddell was said to be suffering. There was evidence both from the box into which used and unused diamorphine ampoules were placed and from back calculations based on the post mortem toxicological results that a much larger dose than that which was necessary to prevent pain was contained in that injection. Moreover, he predicted that death was imminent, as, indeed, it turned out to be. However, by the conclusion of all the expert evidence at Dr Moor's trial for the murder of Mr Liddell at the Newcastle Crown Court in May 1999, the evidence of back calculation based on the amount of diamorphine in Mr Liddell's body was not sufficiently reliable to be left to the jury as a sure basis for determining the strength of the injection. However, there was still the evidence of the 'boasting,' lies in interview by an NHS executive when he maintained that he had not given any injection at all on the morning of death, obfuscation to the Police by referring to intramuscular injections of Largactyl only and the 'missing,' unused diamorphine ampoules, all of which pointed to a deliberate overdose to 'cause a peaceful death.' After being charged, Dr Moor admitted having given the mixed injection but claimed it contained a modest amount of diamorphine; he also claimed he had not intended to hasten death, had never practised euthanasia and had been significantly misquoted in media reports. At trial he denied any intention to assist death, asserting he had only injected a small amount of diamorphine consistent with relieving pain and which would not be expected to compromise respiration. The jury was directed that, in order to convict of murder (and no other verdict was available to them) they had to be sure that Dr Moor caused the patient's death by the administration of an 'overdose' of diamorphine on the morning of his death and that his purpose in giving the drug was not to give treatment which he believed in the circumstances as he understood them to be proper treatment to relieve pain and suffering but his intention was to kill. Within a relatively short space of time the jury acquitted. Why?

Like Dr Harold Shipman,[2] Dr Moor was a very popular GP, trusted by his patients, as was testified to by many witnesses. Mr Liddell's daughter, and probably the patient himself, requested that he should not suffer. The medical evidence called by the defence, supported by the observations of attending nurses, was that Mr Liddell was, in any event, very close to death and may have died from heart failure (as opposed to morphine poisoning). Although Dr Moor's actions were unusual and contrary to established practice, the precise amount of diamorphine that he injected could not be proved. The jury probably concluded that, although he may well have intended to cause the patient's death having originally boasted that was his indeed intention, they could not be sure he had, and that even if he had, death was imminent and, as a result of Dr Moor's actions, pain-free. Experience of acquittals by juries is that in many cases, particularly when the consequences of conviction are severe (in this case life imprisonment), they reach what they consider to be the 'just' conclusion on all the facts known to them rather than a strict application of the law. Every member of the jury brings their own experiences and 'emotional baggage' with them. Were Dr Moor to have been tried after the case of Dr Shipman, I suspect the outcome may have been different; first, much was learnt in the investigation and presentation of the evidence in the case of Dr Moor which assisted in the later case of Dr Shipman and, secondly, public awareness of the approach of some doctors, particularly sole practitioners, in this area has been significantly heightened by that notorious case.[3]

Notes

1. Central Criminal Court 9 April 1957.

2. See chapter 8.

3. Dr Moor was an alcoholic; he ceased practising when the Police investigation began and died not long after his acquittal.

Part 1

The Fox and the Foetus

"... abortion is a plague of pandemic proportions. Modern medicine has made giant strides in prolonging life and curing disease, especially in children. Is it not ironic that the biggest killer of all remains unchecked?

"EFRAT Organization has been dealing with the problem of abortion since 1977. Over the years we have saved tens of thousands of lives. After hearing thousands of stories, and dealing with women of all sorts, we have made an amazing discovery. *Never,* in all the years, have we encountered a woman who regretted maintaining her pregnancy. Once their babies were born, their mothers were thrilled with them, and rejoiced in them.

"This fact is a very powerful one, and should be noted by professionals dealing with these issues. No other medical procedure, which a woman is considering, will enable her to say with perfect sincerity, 'I have no regrets!'"

(Dr Eli J. Schussheim, President, EFRAT)

Chapter 1

The Fox and the Foetus

"We published a cartoon recently that showed a horse dying, and we spent a week responding to complaints."
(Daniel Finkelstein, Associate Editor of *The Times*)[1]

We live in a time where people seem more concerned with the welfare of animals than they are with the life of children. Incidents of child abuse, both physical and sexual, are increasing alarmingly.[2] Moreover, the rate of abortion in the West is beyond all proportion. Yet in recent years Parliament legislated to outlaw fox hunting with hounds. The debate on fox hunting that led up to the new legislation proved to be one of the lengthiest debates in recent history running into many hundreds of hours. Many members of Parliament were clearly emotional when they implored their fellow MPs to wake up to the cruelty endured by foxes. We find that the fluffy fox with his beady and tearful eyes attracts more compassion than the scan of the child sucking his thumb in the womb – society is concerned with the life of the former yet the life of the latter is discarded and incinerated along with the rest of the hospital waste. Yes, strong language but the truth. This is also a tragedy in that we would rather not hear the blunt reality of what goes on behind closed doors. We appear more concerned with what we say and how we say it than with what we do. In addition, there is a lack of awareness and debate about the true sense of morality and right and wrong that should underpin our actions.

I recall that in the 1980s two comedians, Hale and Pace, performed their infamous sketch of the 'Pet Shop.' The two comedians entered their pet shop and wreaked havoc. They took what were clearly pretend animals and destroyed them – they placed a fake cat in a microwave and squashed a pretend turtle. The BBC received an unprecedented level of complaints. Britain is a country of animal lovers. Daniel Finkelstein reports that his paper spent a week replying to complaints about a *cartoon* that contained an image of a dying horse. Significant sections of society are deluded into thinking that because they care for and have compassion for animals they are somehow good, even though so many children continue to suffer. Is it better to sponsor a donkey in a sanctuary or restore someone's sight in Africa? Dame Elizabeth Butler-Sloss in The Paul Sieghart Memorial Lecture said:

> "It is however well known that the RSPCA and the PDSA receive vastly more money than the NSPCC. We give more for donkey sanctuaries than for children in need. We have a donkey sanctuary in Devon with a counterpart on the island of Lamu off the Kenyan coast. The English donkey home does not know how to spend its money and the farrier visits once a fortnight."[3]

Of course cruelty to animals is abhorrent and unacceptable and this is clear.[4] We must play our part in preventing this but it does not mean that we must remain quiet about the terrible rate of abortion. For more than ten years I have spoken repeatedly – both when I was Rav in Cardiff and also in Leeds – about the shocking treatment of the unborn child. This has provoked uncomfortable reactions amongst some of the audience with a doctor on one occasion walking out of a sermon. But how can any religious or moral person not be moved by the revelation of the sheer level of statistics? 190,000 children aborted in England and Wales each year,[5] 120,000 children aborted each day worldwide and more than 44 million aborted annually.

A gynaecologist told me that he was once called to assist at a centre for the termination of pregnancies in the North of England. A woman had just had a termination and was bleeding to death. The gynaecologist turned up with his colleagues in the ambulance and as they led the lady away on the stretcher the director of the organisation said reassuringly to the doctors:

> "You know, over the last thirty years we have performed 120,000 abortions in this clinic and never once lost a life."

The doctors were shocked, not only at the sheer scale of the number of abortions that had been performed there but that the director had no feeling or conscience for the lives that he *had* terminated and thereby lost; 120,000 of them. Has society become so hardened that we have lost sight of the magnitude of the horror? Too many people are more concerned with the fox than the foetus.

I lament that more people do not raise these issues. I lament further the fact that more people feel uncomfortable when this issue is raised and they would rather rabbis spoke about 'less controversial matters' – maybe tephillin (phylacteries) is a safer bet to discuss.[6] Judaism has something to say about everything, not just actions between man and God but equally about actions between man and his fellow. Judaism has a view on every area of human life and the world at large. Halachah was built on debate, yet today we seem afraid of debate.

Notes

1. Daniel Finkelstein, Associate Editor of *The Times, The Jewish Chronicle,* 17 February 2006.

2. www.nspcc.org.uk.

3. Dame Elizabeth Butler-Sloss, DBE, President of the Family Division, The Paul Sieghart Memorial Lecture, *"Are we failing the family? Human rights, children and the meaning of family in the 21st century,"* British Institute of Human Rights, King's College London, 3 April 2003, www.judiciary.gov.uk.

4. Judaism abhors foxhunting for pleasure or for sport. The Jewish view was articulated by Rabbi Y. Landau (1713-1793) "I am amazed by this activity [hunting]; we have not found hunters in the Torah except for Nimrod and Esau. This is not the way of the sons of Abraham, Isaac and Jacob … it is written 'His [G-d's] mercy is upon all His creatures' … if so how can an Israelite kill living beings, without any other need than in order to pass his time by hunting! This matter contributes to cruelty, and is forbidden …" *Responsa Noda Biyhudah* YD 10.

5. Department of Health Statistics, www.dh.gov.uk/en/Publicationsand statistics/Publications/PublicationsStatistics/DH_4136852.

6. I have long said that although many people say that they want their rabbi to be up to speed with current affairs, if indeed they are up to speed, some feel threatened since it means that Judaism and Torah values are relevant at all times and therefore the listener must modify his practice. As a result, these same people then revert to wanting the rabbi to talk about more traditional issues (probably tephillin-phylacteries) which enables them to continue to propose that Judaism remains irrelevant to them in the twenty-first century.

Chapter 2

Passive Immorality

"Passive smoking kills – so does passive immorality."

I thought of a sentence to highlight the moral problems of our time, 'Clint puffs, shoots and shoots and is prosecuted.' What does it mean? Just like a sentence in which the wrong punctuation makes it incomprehensible, so too, information without background does not make sense.[1] Clint puffs his cigarette, kills the foetus and administers a lethal injection to a dying patient. What is he prosecuted for? – Not for aborting the foetus and not for killing the patient but for smoking in public! Such would be the case in some countries today.

Whilst I welcome measures to prevent harm through passive smoking, when we compare and contrast smoking with abortion of the unborn child or euthanasia, it illustrates the distortion of moral and ethical direction which we face.

The argument that the Jewish community should keep its head down and not draw attention to itself by disseminating Torah views is a weak argument. Maimonides explains that we have an obligation to teach Gentiles the Seven Noachide Laws, namely:

1. Prohibition on idolatry (*Avodah Zarah*).
2. Prohibition on blasphemy and cursing the Name of God (*Birkat HaShem*).
3. Prohibition on murder (*Shefichat Damim*).
4. Prohibition on robbery and theft (*Gezel*).
5. Prohibition on immorality and forbidden sexual relations *(Gilui Arayot).*
6. Prohibition on removing and eating a limb from a live animal (*Eiver Min HaChai*).
7. A requirement to establish a system of justice and courts of law to enforce the other six laws (*Dinim*).

Men and women are equal in their responsibility to observe the Seven Noachide Laws. The Jewish People have an obligation to teach Gentiles these laws. The Late Lubavitcher Rebbe, Rabbi M. M. Schneerson (1902-1994) said:

"The Jew has a crucial role to play in this. He cannot be a bystander, remaining aloof from the world's conduct. Maimonides rules, '... Moses our teacher instructed [the Jewish people], [having been authorised] from the mouth of God, to convince all the inhabitants of the world to observe the commandments given to the children of Noah.'[2] It is the Jew's duty to see to it that *all* peoples lead the righteous and decent life which comes from compliance with the Seven Noachide Laws.

"Not only is it a Jew's duty because he has been so commanded by God, but it is also to his own benefit. A world full of chaos, where nations and individuals live by no law except that dictated by self-interest, must inevitably affect the Jew."[3]

Some years ago, when I was Rav in Cardiff, the then Bishop of Monmouth and now Archbishop of Canterbury, Dr Rowan Williams, spoke in our synagogue hall to the Council of Christian and Jews (CCJ). Following his talk, I asked him whether he was aware that Maimonides requires Jews to teach Gentiles the Seven Noachide Laws, and what he thought about this? His reply was interesting and honest, he said something on these lines, "I suppose since the Jews had been persecuted by the Church the persecutors would hardly have been interested to know the views of those they were persecuting and what they may be required to teach them!"

Thank God, today the Church does not persecute us and since we live in a free and democratic country we are able to express our political and religious views without fear of oppression. As such, I say to those who argue that we should remain quiet and not draw attention to ourselves that they are wholly misguided. We must speak up, for it is our obligation to do so.

Moreover, we must be conscious of the fact that whilst Western values promote individualism this is in contradistinction to Jewish religious belief. Judaism teaches that whatever actions the individual undertakes, they do not take place in a vacuum, but rather they affect their family, community, city, country and ultimately the entire world. This theory is popularised today through Edward Lorenz's 1963 description of the 'butterfly effect': the possibility that a large storm in Indonesia may be caused by a butterfly flapping its wings in Australia.

Therefore, just like recent legislation in the UK has outlawed smoking in public places due to the harmful effects of passive smoking, so too, we must be conscious of the similarly lethal effects of passive immorality. We should adopt the mind-set that what others undertake *does* impact on me and I can advocate through debate, discussion and teaching the Jewish/religious view on these subjects.

Consider the issues grouped together in the table below:

Tolerated by Society	Not Tolerated by Society
Abortion	Fox Hunting
Obese Children[4]	Obese Dogs[5]
Gay Partnerships	Political Incorrectness
Sexual Activity in a (secluded) Public Place	Smoking in a Public Place

Whilst the above are not intended to be pairs per se, they do emphasise quite starkly, when grouped together, a moral distortion or lack of moral emphasis. And just as I have stated previously that fox hunting as a sport and smoking in public places should be banned, so too I stress here that political correctness has an important place in a tolerant multi-cultural society in the same way that dogs must be properly cared for. But I feel that these have become smokescreens, or issues that give us a false sense of satisfaction that we are being moral, good and tolerant. Rather, we need to take a broader view and examine other moral issues currently allowed in Western society and ask where are we really heading?

In this connection, it is worth recalling that the first comprehensive and methodical attempt to pass legislation governing the preservation of the animal kingdom and the natural world was by the Nazi regime. Indeed, the first law passed through the Reichstag was a law outlawing Shechitah – the ritual slaughter of animals. While this does not detract from the importance of protecting the environment, it does illustrate that the love of nature and hatred of human beings are not necessarily contradictory in some people's eyes. In the words of the Prophet Hosea: "They that sacrifice men kiss calves."[6]

Hitler played heavily on the anti-Semitism latent in his people. He blamed the Jews for two great wounds upon humanity: circumcision on the body and conscience on the soul. Hitler said that Jews brought conscience and that he would rid the world of conscience. Are we, through our silence, to allow Hitler's wishes to come true?

Notes

1. There is an interesting book on English grammar by Lynne Truss, *Eats Shoots and Leaves*. If the comma is placed after "eats" it distorts the entire meaning of the sentence.

2. *Mishneh Torah, Laws of Kings* 8:10.

3. *Sichos in English,* 11th Nissan 5743-1983, volume 16 p. 298.

4. In February 2007 an overweight 8 year-old set off a debate on child obesity in Britain. Connor McCreaddie, of Wallsend, northeastern England, weighed at the time 218 pounds (98 kg), four times the weight of a healthy child his age. Connor and his mother, Nicola McKeown, 35, both attended a child protection meeting with North Tyneside Council officials. Afterwards, the Local Safeguarding Children Board issued a brief statement saying that it was able to confirm that its hope and ambition was to enable this child to remain with his family. They said, "In order to move this matter forward we have made a formal agreement with the family to safeguard and promote the child's welfare." The agency provided no details about what McCreaddie or his mother would have to do to fight his obesity. The hearing was held under the Children Act, which places a duty on the local authority to conduct an inquiry if it has "reasonable cause to suspect that a child … in their area is suffering, or is likely to suffer, significant harm." The boy's case attracted national attention after his mother allowed an ITV News crew to film his day-to-day life over the course of a month. The mother who had feared that she might lose custody of her obese 8 year-old son unless he lost weight was allowed to keep the boy after striking a deal with social workers to safeguard his welfare. It should be noted however, that whereas in the case of the pet Labrador (see next footnote) the dog was taken into care and immediately helped by losing weight the child remains obese. Moreover, the case about the dog went to the courts and local authority before the case of the child: how can this be?

5. In January 2007 in an unprecedented case, David and Derek Benton were prosecuted by the RSPCA because Rusty, their pet Labrador, was 116 pounds (74 kg), more than double the weight he should have been. They denied causing unnecessary suffering to the 10 year-old dog but were found guilty by magistrates in Ely, Cambridgeshire. They were given a conditional discharge for three years and ordered

to pay £250 costs each. Rusty had been taken into the care of the RSPCA and had lost three and a half stone since March after being put on a low-calorie diet and given painkilling drugs costing £3,000. The prosecution incurred legal costs of £12,000.

6. *Hosea* 13:2.

Chapter 3

A Time to Speak

"There is a time for everything … a time to speak."
(Ecclesiastes)[1]

I mentioned in the previous chapter the responsibility we have as Jews to disseminate the view of the Torah. I wish to develop this a little more. In a question and answer session after one of my talks, one lady remarked politely as follows. "Those who are religious will ask their rabbi what they should do concerning assisted dying and those who are irreligious won't, so what do you hope to achieve with your talk?"

I would highlight the following points in response:

- People must be sufficiently informed with the relevant basics of halachah on a given subject, so that they may be in a position to put the facts clearly to their rabbi.
- Even those who may be sympathetic to halachic values and who even abide by them must also strengthen their belief.
- We have an obligation to spread the word, especially on key issues such as life and death, to other Jews and to society as a whole, something which for example the Chief Rabbi Sir Jonathan Sacks has done on a

range of issues via *The Times*, *The Guardian* and BBC's *Thought For The Day*.

- In a letter to *The Times*[2] the Archbishop of Canterbury, the Archbishop of Westminster and the Chief Rabbi united collectively to condemn Lord Joffe's Assisted Dying for the Terminally Ill Bill. Faith leaders have entered the debate, so must we as faith individuals.

- In my discussions with two ministers from Zurich, Switzerland, Rabbi Dr Zalman Kossowsky (Av Beth Din) and Rabbi Marcel Ebel (Chaplain to Hospitals) explained that the Chaplain speaks to people who may be contemplating assisted dying to explain, in an appropriate manner, the severity of the halachah on this issue. They highlighted that they have had some success in changing people's minds. Clearly, it is the rabbi who must often take the initiative and approach the person or family. We should be encouraged by their success and attempt to make similar moves in appropriate areas where halachic values may be challenged.

Rabbi Joseph Horowitz (1848-1920), known as the Alter of Navardok,[3] emphasises the need for each person to be aware of the erosion of morals in society and to endeavour to make a difference.[4] He writes: "We see the power of self-commitment to be so great as to enable the individual, with rightness of intent, genuineness of deed and strength of spirit, to be, as it were, like a locomotive which pulls many carriages after it. In like manner, he, by whole-hearted 'pulling,' can turn the whole world back whence they had strayed."[5] So, we should not think that the little we do is irrelevant. On the contrary, it is all valuable and makes a huge difference.

Secular Western thinking which believes that "as long as I do not interfere with the way someone else chooses to live their life and they do not adversely impinge on my life, we may all co-exist peacefully," has influence on us. However, this is not the Torah view. It is for this reason that I reiterate why I compiled this book, to create constructive debate and impress upon readers the Torah approach.

I have often led discussions with groups of people of different ages and from different points on the religious spectrum and asked them what they consider to be absolutely morally wrong. It has frequently been difficult to find a point on which all agree. If we take murder and adultery as two serious sins, people will argue that there are times when murder is understood and circumstances when people tolerate or justify adultery. The area that all people consider wrong in all circumstances is paedophilia. It is frightening that this often tends to be the *only* issue where people are united in their abhorrence and are not able to have a consensus on other areas. This is symptomatic of the lack of clarity of boundaries in society and the need therefore to explore ways of remedying this from a Torah perspective.

Notes

1. 3:7.

2. *The Times,* 12 May 2006.

3. He wrote an influential work on the importance of introspection and responsibility called *Madregat Ha'Adam* (*The Stature of Man*). Chapter four is dedicated *To Turn the Many to Righteousness.*

4. *Madregat Ha'Adam, Mezakeh Ha'Rabim, To Turn the Many to Righteousness,* translated by Shraga Silverstein, (Jerusalem: Feldheim), 4:1.

5. Ibid. 4:7.

Part 2

The Fatal Injection

"Murder is an act or series of acts ... which were intended to kill and did in fact kill the dead woman. It does not matter for this purpose that her death was inevitable and her days were numbered. If her life was cut short by weeks or months it is just as much murder as if it were cut short by years ... It remains the law that no doctor nor any man, no more in the case of a dying man than the healthy, has the right to deliberately cut the thread of life."

(Mr Justice Devlin, April 1957)

Introduction

"Perhaps the easiest way of explaining it is that things that are sacrosanct are not ours to do with as we wish. The environment is one. Personal dignity is another. Human life is a third. The wisdom of the ages has taught us not to regard these things as if they were our personal possessions. Why? The self-professed agnostic Friedrich Hayek explained it best in his last book *The Fatal Conceit* ... the law of unintended consequences, which says that whatever you foresee as the result of your choice is only a small part of the story. Decisions have ripples of consequence no one can predict at the time."

"To legalise assisted dying is fraught with dangers, chief of which is the deconsecration of life. The history of societies that have sanctioned euthanasia in the past is not an encouraging one. In part, Judaism and Christianity were protests against ages in which human life was held dispensable and disposable.

"Those who propose the current Bill do so from the highest of motives. But purity of motive has never ensured rightness of outcomes; often it has been the reverse. To give the dying dignity, using all possible means to treat their pain is one thing. To allow medically assisted suicide is another. If we lose our reverence for human life we will one day lose much else besides."

(Chief Rabbi Sir Jonathan Sacks)[1]

In 2003, in the UK Lord Joffe lodged a Private Member's Bill for Assisted Dying for the Terminally Ill. Essentially, the Bill, had it become law, would have allowed doctors to hasten the death of patients suffering from terminal illnesses and allow them to hand patients lethal drugs to enable dying patients to commit suicide. On 12 May 2006 the Bill had its second reading in the House of Lords and this time round it was defeated. I stress this time round, because it is my belief that, as with many other bills, they are redrafted and governments are pressured until they accept them in one form or other. I believe that this is not a pessimistic outlook but rather a realistic outlook. Doctors George, Finlay and Jeffrey writing in the British Medical Journal state that

> "… the *chameleon of euthanasia continues to change*, and the current shade is physician assisted suicide. The politically correct position for clinicians is 'studied neutrality' since doctors will not really be involved in assisted suicide."[2]

This confirms the very real fear that proposals to change the law will be changed and changed again until it is sufficiently palatable and thereby possible to be implemented.[3]

A number of television documentaries and dramas have recently incorporated the notion of assisted dying. The popular British BBC drama Holby City ran a story in late 2006 of a lady, suffering from motor neurone disease, who went to Switzerland to die in an assisted dying clinic. Each stage of the process was shown quite graphically. The All Party Parliamentary Group on Dying Well, which is currently chaired by Baroness Finlay of Llandaff, posted an article on their website condemning this episode. They argued that "the subject was handled in a wholly one-sided manner."[4]

Whilst this episode of Holby City will have shocked some, it will also have desensitised others, thereby making assisted dying more palatable. Moreover, it will have re-ignited the debate amongst the general populace as to the suitability and acceptability of such legislation here in the United Kingdom. This section now deals with the issues related to the Assisted Dying Bill.

The following definitions are clarified here within the context of this book (these definitions are generally used by writers when discussing these issues but not necessarily by all[5]):

Assisted Dying: someone else provides barbiturates to a person wishing to die, but it is the patient who actually takes them.

(Voluntary) Euthanasia: someone else, for example a doctor, actually administers a lethal drug that terminates the life of another person.

It must be further noted that in some countries where assisted dying is legal, in just under *one in five cases* the barbiturates do not work and a doctor administers a lethal injection to terminate fully the person's life.[6]

Notes

1. Chief Rabbi Sir Jonathan Sacks, *The Jewish Tradition Is Firmly Opposed To Assisted Dying, The Times,* 6 May 2006.

2. R. J. D. George, I. G. Finlay and D. Jeffrey *Legalised Euthanasia Will Violate the Rights of Vulnerable Patients*, BMJ, Volume 331, 24 September 2005, p. 684.

3. The new 2005 Bill is available on the UK Parliament website. It contains the text of the Assisted Dying for the Terminally Ill Bill, as ordered to be printed in the House of Lords on 9 November 2005,

www.publications.parliament.uk/pa/ld200506/ldbills/036/2006036. htm. The previous 2004 Bill, on which the Select Committee Report was based, is still available for comparison. It contains the text of the Assisted Dying for the Terminally Ill Bill, as introduced in the House of Lords on 8 January 2004, www.publications.parliament.uk/pa/ld200304/ldbills/017/2004017.htm.

4. For the full critique of this episode of Holby City see www.dyingwell.org.uk *Assisted Dying and Holby City.*

5. For more terms and meanings see *Definitions of Euthanasia*, Derek Humphry, 19 January 2006, www.assisted.suicide.org.

6. R. J. D. George, I. G. Finlay and D. Jeffrey *Legalised Euthanasia Will Violate the Rights of Vulnerable Patients*, BMJ, volume 331, 24 September 2005, p. 684. They argue with the suggestion that euthanasia and assisted dying are different. They retort, "What doctor prescribing for assisted suicide would refuse to complete it with euthanasia?" Ibid.

Chapter 4

The Fatal Injection

> "By the time you read this I will be dead."
> (Anne Turner aged 66, January 2006)

To talk in a general sense about assisted dying and the issues it raises for the terminally ill is one thing, but in order to appreciate the truly sensitive nature of the matter and the difficulties people face, it is necessary to focus on real life cases. Moreover, this enables us to evaluate some of the arguments put forward on this subject. In this chapter we will also explore Dignitas in Switzerland – a clinic for assisted dying.

Case Study One:

In January 2006 Dr Anne Turner – who was suffering from the incurable brain disease Progressive Supranuclear Palsy (PSP) – hit the headlines when she travelled to Switzerland to end her life at Ludwig Minelli's assisted dying clinic. Before her departure she wrote one hundred letters to family and friends and told them in the letters, "By the time you read this I will be dead." Moreover, through the media attention she attracted she used it to highlight the need for the UK government to legalise assisted dying.

Somewhat ironically she claimed that the government had *caused her to die earlier* than she should have done, since she travelled to Switzerland to terminate her life whilst she was still able to travel. Had she been allowed to do this in the UK she would have stayed alive longer and terminated her life when she was ready. Her logic, though seemingly powerful, is distorted because governments that have legislation forbidding assisted dying and euthanasia cannot be blamed for ending people's lives prematurely.

Case Study Two:

In 2006, David March, aged 57, helped his wife commit suicide. She had been suffering from multiple sclerosis. Mrs March, aged 59, of Caterham, Surrey, had tried to kill herself on a number of occasions because of her ill health.

Mr March returned home to find Mrs March in a wheelchair, having taken valium and with a plastic bag over her head. He admitted to police that he tightened a string around the bag and that she died half an hour after he arrived. But his plea to the lesser offence of aiding and abetting her suicide was accepted after a pathologist said it was not certain that Mrs March would have survived if he had not tightened the string. He walked free from court with a nine-month suspended prison sentence.

Passing sentence at the Old Bailey, Judge Brian Barker told March: "You were a husband who not only had a deep love for his wife but who displayed a selfless devotion to her. Society may understand your acts but cannot condone them."

Whilst the sentence was welcomed by the pressure group Dignity In Dying, the British Council of Disabled People said: "What kind of message is this sending out to society where it is perceived to be easier to kill a disabled person rather than support them to live with dignity?"[1]

Dignitas

In Switzerland, assisted dying is legal. Ludwig Minelli lives in a quiet suburb of Zurich; he is in his seventies. In 1998, he founded Dignitas, the clinic for assisted dying. As of early 2006 he had assisted more than 450 people to commit suicide.[2] Minelli makes what he believes to be an important distinction between assisted dying and euthanasia. In euthanasia, the doctor performs the last act in helping a patient to die whereas in assisted dying, the patients must perform the final act themselves, usually by drinking a lethal concoction. This consists of 12 grams of sodium pentobarbital mixed with a glass of water. The person's last act will involve taking a drink from this glass. Then they will lie down, and after five minutes will fall into a deep coma. Twenty to thirty minutes later they will die.

Many of his 5,500 members are suffering from terminal illnesses, but others have non-terminal conditions such as osteoporosis, epilepsy or mental illnesses. Minelli believes that everyone has the right to choose to die.

But he does not stop here. Minelli wants his work to take on a 'new direction.' He wants to make the option of assisted suicide available to a far wider group of people – to the mentally ill and those with illnesses that are not in themselves life-threatening. He believes that everyone should have the right to kill themselves, and that if that 'taboo' is lifted, the incidence of bungled para-suicides and painful suicides will decrease.[3]

Minelli has fallen down the slippery slope, advocating not only the taking of life for those in great pain but also for all who, for whatever reason, are contemplating suicide to end their lives in his clinic. It may be that Minelli's intentions are honourable, but purity of motive does not ensure a righteous or moral outcome. The astonishing ramifications of his ideas will be considered a far cry from what even the original proponents of assisted dying in

Switzerland first envisaged.

However, this comes as no surprise. It echoes the problems now endured in the UK since the Abortion Act 1967. Then, the proponents of the Act were concerned, amongst other things, about 'back street abortions' and anticipated that fewer women would be harmed if allowed to abort their children in a safe medical environment. Moreover, it was intended to restrict the number of terminations. However, in reality, more and more women found themselves with 'unwanted pregnancies' which has led to record numbers of abortions. As the provisions of the Act are widely ignored the number of abortions mainly carried out in NHS hospitals has continued to rise. This easy access to abortion has reduced vigilance in the use of contraception and led to the readily available 'lunch-time abortions.'

There is a pervasive belief that some Eskimos left their elderly on the ice to die. This is not altogether true. It is true that sometimes elderly Eskimos who could no longer hunt or do other useful work might choose, or be persuaded to choose, a form of assisted suicide when food was very scarce. In fact, they were not left to die on the ice, but rather were more directly dispatched. But this practice was not universal among the Eskimo people – some bands of Eskimo never had such practices – and it was only tolerated under truly desperate conditions. Respected elders largely ruled Eskimo communities, and routine geronticide did not take place. A far more common response to desperate conditions and the threat of starvation was infanticide, which did sometimes entail abandoning an infant in the hope that someone less desperate might find and adopt it before the cold or the wildlife killed it.[4]

I cannot help but feel that if not for the liberal attitudes in the West today, the West would view the Eskimos as primitive uncivilised people. Yet the West, from a so-called civilised perspective, holds very similar views which are mass levels of abortion and moves toward senilicide and even infanticide. At the risk of sounding cynical, I would say that until a view is adopted by Western thinking it is considered primitive and when adopted by the West it becomes a 'civilised' approach.

Notes

1. Stewart Payne, *An Act of Love*, www.telegraph.co.uk, 21 October 2006.

2. This number is constantly increasing.

3. Jocasta Shakespeare, *A Date With Death, The Sunday Times,* 16 April 2006.

4. www.crystalinks.com/inuit.html.

Chapter 5

Medical Opinions

"Kill this Bill which is a Licence to Kill."
(Lord (Robert) Winston)[1]

Common sense suggests that humane people would be revolted by euthanasia and assisted dying and that they would side with victims such as severely handicapped babies whose lives have been terminated or risk being terminated. But that is not what happens. What happens is that liberals struggle to make sense of this termination of life. They feel that a horrible act must have some reason. They search for the source of the desperation that drove the person to end their life and seek to justify the termination of babies' lives. Instead of supporting the victim, they end up siding with the murderer. It appears that the worse the act of violence, the stronger the impulse to understand!

Amongst the numerous articles written for and against assisted dying in the UK, there are many eminent professors, leading ethicists and doctors doing just that – finding reasoned arguments and ethical and moral standpoints to justify the active termination of someone's life. During the years 2005 and 2006, the British Medical Journal (BMJ) ran a series of articles on the subject of assisted dying. The Journal presented a viewpoint with both sides of the argument discussed and writers were given the opportunity to explore this subject from medical, philosophical and moral perspectives. Here are some of the main arguments against assisted dying (not necessarily from a Jewish viewpoint but from a secular viewpoint as well):

- The sanctity of life is under threat[2]
- To hasten the death of a patient regardless of motive is akin to murder[3]
- Life is God given, and when terminated by man, a person is considered is if he has fought God[4]
- If we lose our reverence for human life we will one day lose much else besides[5]
- Slippery slope[6]
- Strong-willed people will pressure the vulnerable
- People who want to live but feel that they are a burden will have their lives terminated
- Termination of life might be against patients' wishes
- The Bill is seen by disabled groups in particular as being anti-equality and anti-social[7]
- It would socially invalidate the life of the suffering individual[8]
- Old people will see themselves as a burden on their family and healthcare system and therefore they will feel under pressure (real or imagined) to die[9]
- Vulnerable people could feel under pressure to opt for suicide[10]
- Confused elderly people might believe that the law introduced a presumption that life should be ended[11]
- It could imply a duty to die[12]
- Once promoted to a medical good, therapeutic killing becomes a legitimate consideration in resource management, for example, to free hospital beds[13]
- Palliative care will be diminished for those who want it

- People who are not in a position to express a wish to die may have that decision made for them
- Therapeutic killing of children, people with psychiatric illness and the mentally incapable[14]
- What happens when there is a lack of consensus amongst doctors and family?
- Doctors are largely against such legislation[15]
- It would diminish trust between patients and members of the medical profession[16]
- It would have a profound effect on clinical codes, duties and practice of doctors and nurses[17]
- In some countries where this has become law, therapeutic killing without consent has become laudable and morally necessary[18]
- Emotional impact on doctors, nurses and family members who agree to assisted dying[19]
- Doctors worry about being insufficiently prepared should they be confronted by these issues[20]
- Doctors are concerned for their reputations[21]
- Moral cost on society[22]
- Healers should not be those who assist their patients' self-destruction[23]
- Decisions have ripples of consequence which no one can predict at the time[24]

These are some of the secular arguments in favour of assisted dying:

- Greater respect for personal autonomy[25]
- The right to die[26]
- The 'right to life' does not mean bare existence, it means existence that has a certain minimum quality[27]
- When consensus is lacking courts are the appropriate place to decide what is needed[28]
- Clear legal parameters will protect people
- Review procedures may protect people[29]

- To do away with doctors' paternalism towards patients
- Conscientious objection of doctors' own values should not be a factor[30]
- To relieve suffering
- Public opinion is in favour[31]
- Medicine has prolonged not only lives but periods of dying[32]
- People find it humiliating to have to continue living, experiencing mental and physical decay[33]
- It would mean that people may approach the terminal phase of their lives without fear and that they have a way out[34]
- Why should people be forced to go abroad for such services?
- Minority religious groups should not impose their views on the majority
- Legislation will prevent prosecutions against well-meaning family members who currently help assist the death of a relative[35]

There is an ironic argument currently posited by those in favour of euthanasia. Deborah Annetts, the chief executive of Dignity in Dying, formerly known as the Voluntary Euthanasia Society, described cases of people having to travel abroad for example to Switzerland as "truly heartbreaking." She said that the Government must make time in Parliament for the Assisted Dying for the Terminally Ill Bill because if this Bill would become law people would not have been forced to go to Zurich whilst they were still able to travel for help to die. Some would still be alive today. "Our law is shortening rather than prolonging life."[36]

A similar view has been expressed by MEP Chris Davies who has said that it is "cruel and heartless" that British law against assisted suicide should force people to travel abroad to end their pain.[37]

These views lay the blame on society and the government for not allowing people to terminate their lives in the UK; instead they travel abroad to terminate their lives whilst they are still able to, rather than dying later in the UK when their illness will have progressed to a more debilitating stage. This argument simply does not hold water because from a religious perspective, whether here or abroad, the prohibition to actively terminate a life remains. This turning of tables to create a feeling of guilt on those opposed to assisted dying is simply another tool in this peculiar notion that terminating a life is somehow an act of compassion.

Up-to-Date View of the British Medical Association (BMA)

In 2005, the BMA made a controversial attempt to remain neutral on the subject of assisted dying. An overwhelming majority later reversed this decision. On 29 June 2006 at the annual conference doctors voted as follows:

British Medical Association

1. Improvement in Palliative Care – 84% in favour and 16% against
2. Physician Assisted Suicide and Voluntary Euthanasia – two thirds against and one third in favour
3. Involuntary Euthanasia for Patients Who Cannot Make a Decision – 94% against and 6% in favour
4. For a Clear Demarcation between Doctors Against and in Favour Should the Law Ever Be Passed – 82% in favour and 18% against

---

Dr Michael Wilks, the chairman of the BMA Ethics Committee, said after the debate:

"The BMA's position is now one of opposition to any further legislation. These decisions were made by a carefully elected body that represents the grass roots feeling of the profession. The message was very clear."[38]

Notes

1. Lord (Robert) Winston, *Kill This Bill Which is a Licence to Kill, The Jewish Chronicle,* 17 March 2006, p.34.

2. Ibid.

3. Ibid.

4. Rabbi S. Wagschal, *The Halachos of Aveilus*, (Feldheim: Jerusalem, 1990), p. 2. He basis this on two verses, "*G-d* takes and sustains life" (Samuel 1:2,6) and "... and *You* sustain them all"(Nehemiah 9:6).

5. Chief Rabbi Sir Jonathan Sacks, *The Jewish Tradition Is Firmly Opposed To Assisted Dying, The Times,* 6 May 2006.

6. This means that whatever legislation is drafted, it will either be abused or further modified (often without the general public appreciating these further modifications) thereby extending it beyond the original agreed parameters.

7. Tim McSharry, Access Committee for Leeds, Organisation of Disabled People, Mariners Resource Centre, *The Yorkshire Evening Post,* 13 May 2006, p.12.

8. Ibid.

9. Dr Rowan Williams, Cardinal Cormac Murphy-O'Connor and Sir Jonathan Sacks in a letter to *The Times,* 12 May 2006, p.22 and Lord (Robert) Winston *Kill This Bill Which is a Licence to Kill, The Jewish Chronicle,* 17 March 2006, p. 34.

10. A Communicate Research poll commissioned by the Care Not Killing Alliance, an umbrella group of organisations opposed to euthanasia, found the public to be wary of the Bill on the grounds that it would give the green light for abuse. 65% of people believed that "vulnerable people could feel under pressure to opt for suicide" if the law goes ahead (28% disagreed and 6% said they did not know), www.carenotkilling.org.uk.

11. Michael Portillo, *In Life or Death Decisions, a Legal Muddle Can Help, The Sunday Times,* 14 March 2006 p. 21.

12. R. J. D. George, I. G. Finlay and D. Jeffrey, *Legalised Euthanasia Will Violate the Rights of Vulnerable Patients*, BMJ, volume 331, 24 September 2005, p. 684.

13. Ibid. p. 685.

14. Ibid. p. 684.

15. BMA Annual Conference, 29 June 2006.

16. Dr Rowan Williams, Cardinal Cormac Murphy-O'Connor and Sir Jonathan Sacks in a letter to *The Times,* 12 May 2006, p.22.

17. R J D George, I G Finlay and David Jeffrey, *Legalised Euthanasia Will Violate the Rights of Vulnerable Patients*, BMJ, volume 331, 24 September 2005, p. 684.

18. Ibid. p. 684.

19. Ann Somerville, *Changes in BMA Policy on Assisted Dying*, BMJ, volume 331, 24 September 2005, p. 688.

20. Ibid. p. 687.

21. Ibid.

22. R. J. D. George, I. G. Finlay and D. Jeffrey, *Legalised Euthanasia Will Violate the Rights of Vulnerable Patients*, BMJ, volume 331, 24 September 2005, p. 684.

23. Trevor Stammers, *The Times,* 12 May 2006, p. 22.

24. Chief Rabbi Sir Jonathan Sacks, *The Jewish Tradition Is Firmly Opposed To Assisted Dying, The Times,* 6 May 2006.

25. Torbjorn Tannsjo *Moral Dimensions,* BMJ, volume 331, 24 September 2005, p. 689 and argued by many others as well.

26. Professor A. C. Grayling, *Right to Die,* BMJ, volume 330, 9 April 2005, p. 799.

27. Ibid.

28. Ibid.

29. For a discussion on this see *Dutch Experience of Monitoring Euthanasia,* BMJ, volume 331, 24 September 2005, p. 691-693.

30. Julian Savulescu, *Conscientious Objection in Medicine,* BMJ, volume 332, 4 February 2006, p. 294.

31. M. A. Branthwaite, *Taking The Final Step: Changing The Law on Euthanasia and Physician Assisted Suicide,* BMJ, volume 331, 24 September 2005, p. 682.

32. Torbjorn Tannsjo, *Moral Dimensions,* BMJ, volume 331, 24 September 2005, p. 689.

33. Ibid. p. 691.

34. Ibid.

35. M. A. Branthwaite, *Taking The Final Step: Changing The Law on Euthanasia and Physician Assisted Suicide,* BMJ, volume 331, 24 September 2005, pp. 682-3. This view is also expressed by Baroness Murphy, *A Dying Shame,* bmanews, 24 March 2007, p. 14.

36. Richard Savill, *By The Time You Read This, I Will Be Dead,* www.telegraph.co.uk, 25 January 2006.

37. Chris Davies (2006) *A Matter of Human Rights.* This view was also expressed by Ann Turner as mentioned above.

38. Celia Hall, *The Daily Telegraph,* 30 June 2006.

Chapter 6

Western Thinking and Autonomy

"The language of morality survives, but without the systematic corpus of beliefs which underlay them."
(Alasdair MacIntyre b. 1929)[1]

Any suggestions in favour of assisted dying and euthanasia are rooted in a secular way of thinking. The crucial point here is the concept of autonomy. The Western belief in autonomy is embedded in Kantian ethics (18th cent.) and Stoicism (3rd cent. BCE).

Ancient Stoic philosophers believed that the ultimate form of autonomy is to end one's life if it is no longer worth living. In addition, if a person's values would be compromised then this too could be deemed reason enough to end one's life.

The Stoics were not simply theists, but monotheists in a very strong sense. They believed in a perfectly moral God who both created the universe and controls every aspect of it. However, for the Stoics humans are not separate from God. They believed that God is part of us, and the reason we have the capacity for rational thought is because that rationality is an aspect of God within us. As such, the autonomous freedom of an individual human is central for the Stoics, but it is not opposed to God's Law: when a human being expresses autonomy, provided they are acting rationally, they are necessarily simultaneously following God's will and God's Law.

This does not mean that anything any human does is in accordance with God's will, rather it is only in accordance with God's will if it is rational, and hence moral. The Stoics believed that morality and reason are perfectly in accord with one another. A moral action will be one that will promote good in the world and avoid evil, and a person should primarily act so as to promote good and avoid evil. However, morality overrides everything else, and if morality can only be maintained by choosing for example pain or death, then one should choose pain or death.

For the Stoics, there are two possible reasons for suicide:

First, and most importantly, the need to look at the moral consequences of staying alive. If it may be deduced rationally that staying alive will promote evil, then it is a person's duty to kill himself. A famous example is the Stoic Roman politician Cato. Cato fought against Julius Caesar in the Civil War and was defeated in 46 BCE. On his defeat he committed suicide, and did so even though he knew that Caesar would pardon him and allow him to resume his life and position in Rome. His reasoning was that Caesar was a tyrant, and for him to stay alive under a tyranny would inevitably involve endorsing and promoting evil. But it is rare that a person would be in Cato's position.

More common is the second reason for suicide, which is based on rationally weighing up all the various things in people's lives that are in accordance with nature (for example, health and pleasure) and against nature (for example, sickness and pain), taking into account that life is one – but only one – of the things in accordance with nature. If that rational calculation shows that by staying alive things contrary to nature outweigh those in accordance with nature, then here too it is a person's duty to kill himself.[2]

Stoicism has influenced society today, but indirectly. The key figure here is Immanuel Kant (1724-1804). It is important to note a crucial fact that Kant and other Enlightenment figures were not developing their ideas in a vacuum, but were arguing for them systematically and rationally, drawing on an ancient tradition of ethical thought.

True ethics, for Kant, can only be autonomous, deriving from the rational acceptance by each individual of the systematic logic that (he argues) ethics entails. That logic involves seeing ethics as something universal, shared among all rational beings. So specifics such as whether one is Greek, Roman or indeed German, male or female, Christian or Jew, slave or free, are irrelevant for Kant, as they were for the Stoics. It also involves treating each rational being as a separate autonomous entity, each free to make decisions for him or herself, provided only that they do not violate the autonomy of other rational beings. Kant believed that because religion is imposed by God and does not come from within the person, it cannot be by definition ethical. It will be explained below that Judaism does not believe in autonomous ethics but rather heteronomous ethics.

But interestingly, Kant himself differed from the Stoics in that he in fact opposed suicide – he argued that it was logically contradictory for a rational autonomous being to will its own destruction. So Kantianism is not in favour of suicide or, what we call today, assisted dying and euthanasia.

Because of 'religious thought,' Kantianism in general did not fully permeate into the general way of thinking. By 'religious thought' in the West this predominantly means the practice of Christianity which seeks to hold onto, at least in particularly crucial areas relating to life and death, the sort of religious (heteronomous) ethics that Kant felt he had disproved. Religious thought believes that there are certain sorts of rules derived externally from the individual (from God), and which should not be violated even if it involves rejecting the autonomy of the individual to choose their own death.

Modern Western ethics, while working largely within a Kantian framework, has inconsistently maintained certain sorts of rules, which are incompatible with a Kantian framework. But as religion and the acceptance of religious traditions recede, then there is an increasing feeling that those rules do not make sense, and there is increased pressure to bring them into line with the general secular ethical framework. This means, among other things, the acceptance of the right to a rationally chosen suicide and, by extension, allowing someone to assist someone else to commit a rationally chosen suicide. Hence the attempts, both here in the UK and elsewhere, to introduce legislation along those lines.

In summary, Kant's major contribution was a general theory of what ethics is. He developed this from the legacy of the Stoics, and this is what was then in turn transmitted to later Western ideology. However, people applying that theory to areas like suicide have come up with different answers from Kant's own. This is because originally Western thinkers generally adopted Kant except where religion had a firm grasp, but now, with a weakening of that hold by religion, certain issues are now being re-visited.

The Stoic – and indeed Kantian – roots are frequently overlooked, and from a Jewish perspective this must be addressed. Chief Rabbi Sir Jonathan Sacks' book *One People* takes as its starting point precisely this mismatch between Enlightenment post-Kantian autonomous ethics and traditional Jewish heteronomous ethics. He argues (quoting Alasdair MacIntyre) that the language of morality survives, but without the systematic corpus of beliefs which underlay them.[3]

Chief Rabbi Sacks refers to the "revolution of consciousness" and encapsulates the problem today most pertinently:

"In the Bible, the supreme virtue is to do that which is right 'in the eyes of God.' To do that which is right in one's own eyes is the paradigm of lawlessness. *Post-Kantian ethics reverses these values.* Mere obedience is inauthentic. Moral agency means to be the author of one's behavioural code.

"From the perspective of the autonomous self, then, halachic existence is inauthentic because it flees from making personal choice the centre of its universe.

"[But] From the perspective of tradition, much of contemporary [Western secular] ethics is inauthentic precisely *because* it makes personal choice the measure of all things."[4]

It is appropriate to end this chapter with the following thought. Rabbi Elchanan Wasserman (1875-1941) writes in the name of Rabbi Eliezer Gordon (1841-1910) that people who do not believe in religion claim that they are 'non-believers' and 'open minded.' However, he argues that this is untrue. The person who claims to be a non-believer may not believe in religion but he does still believe in something. It may be the belief in his inner desires or it may be a conviction in an incorrect ideology. The tendency to believe is deeply entrenched in the human mind and if not channelled in one path will be directed elsewhere. Rabbi Wasserman adds that without religion to temper and gauge a person's behaviour they are at a greater risk of fanaticism.[5] The Torah way of life and belief – in contrast to the autonomous self – provides therefore a controlled spiritual and moral framework within which a person may function responsibly.

Notes

1. Quoted by Chief Rabbi Sir Jonathan Sacks, *One People,* (London: Littman, 1993) p 2.

2. *The Epistles of Seneca,* Epistle no.70, which is on the topic of suicide. Seneca believed that it is not how long you live, but how nobly you live. See also passages from Cicero and Diogenes Laertius about Stoic views on suicide, passages 66 G and H in Long & Sedley's standard collection, *The Hellenistic Philosophers,* (Cambridge, 1987) vol. 1 pp. 424-425. Cato is mentioned in the Seneca letter and is also the speaker in the Cicero passage which was written shortly after Cato's death.

3. Chief Rabbi Sir Jonathan Sacks, *One People,* p. 2.

4. Ibid. p. 158. See also Chief Rabbi Sir Jonathan Sacks, *To Heal a Fractured World,* where he adds that the Bible (Judges 21:25) sees autonomy as anarchy and that it is hard to see how society can survive in the long term under such conditions (p. 124). Later on he writes (based on a profound understanding of T. B. Kiddushin 32b) that heteronomy and autonomy are not opposites, as viewed by Kantians, but rather different stages in moral development, first external orders and then internalised through habituation and study (p. 165).

5. *The Baranovich Haggadah,* adapted and translated by Rabbi Yaakov Blinder, (Israel: Feldheim/Targum, 2001), p. 83.

Chapter 7

Torah View on Autonomy

"The soul of a person is not his own property, rather
the property of the Almighty."
(R' David ben Shlomoh ibn Zimra – Radvaz d.1573)[1]

The Torah forbids self-inflicted harm and teaches the belief
that we do not own our bodies and the following sources
support these beliefs. The prohibition "you shall not
murder"[2] includes the prohibition against killing oneself.[3]
Additionally, the Torah states that "I will seek out your
blood for your souls, I will seek it out from every living
creature and from the hand of man."[4] This is understood as
prohibiting not only killing another, but also taking one's
own life.

When discussing the requirement to flog certain sinners,
the Torah states that no more lashes may be administered
than the prescribed amount.[5] Even a sinner who is to be
punished may not be punished more than the Law permits.
Maimonides (1135/8-1204) states, "It is forbidden to harm
oneself or another."[6] The law is echoed in the Shulchan
Aruch[7] and further fleshed out by Rabbi Shneur Zalman
(1745-1812).[8]

Moreover, the Torah states, "You shall not accept a
ransom for the life of a murderer who is guilty of a capital
crime, he must be put to death."[9] Maimonides crystallises

the principle behind this law: "The court is warned against accepting ransom from a murderer, even if he offers all the money in the world and even if the avenger of blood agrees to let him go free. For the life of the murdered person is not the property of the avenger of blood but the property of God."[10]

Radvaz coined the phrase, "The soul of a person is not his own property, rather the property of the Almighty."[11]

Concerning suicide, Rabbi Y. M. Tucazinsky (20th cent.) makes some very pertinent points:

> "It may even be a greater sin to commit suicide than to murder someone else for several reasons. First by killing himself, a person removes all possibility of repentance. Secondly, death in most circumstances is the greatest atonement for one's sins.[12] However, in a suicide's death a cardinal transgression has been committed rather than expiation. A third reason why Judaism abhors suicide is that the person who takes his own life asserts by this act that he denies the Divine Mastery and ownership of his life, his body and soul. The *wilful suicide* further denies his Divine Creation. Our sages compare the departure of a soul from a human body to a Sefer Torah (Torah Scroll) which has been consumed by fire. Thus, a person who commits suicide can be likened to one who burns a Sefer Torah."[13]

Rabbi S. R. Hirsch (1808-1888) when discussing the beauty of the mitzvah of Shabbat links the lack of autonomy with the concept of the Shabbat covenant:

> "It [Shabbat] is a covenant, the only contract and basis of every relationship between God and the Jew, both as man and as Israelite. For if you consider the world and yourself as God's property, and regard

your power over the earth as lent to you by God for the fulfilment of your task in life, then will your life be lived in accordance with the Torah. But if you regard the world as your own and yourself as its master, then the contract is torn up, and you are just making sport of the Torah."[14]

These powerful words portray the depth and centrality of the absence of the autonomous-self in Judaism, and how through that realisation and acceptance of Divine Mastery over the self, a person is able to serve the Almighty by observing His Law.

The argument that is often put forward in support of assisted dying and euthanasia is that the person is acting out of compassion to relieve pain and suffering, and therefore they do not do not consider their act as one of murder. Such a viewpoint, however well meaning, remains contrary to the Torah view. Pain and quality of life v. life itself are not for us to weigh up and decide upon. Judaism considers the sanctity of life God given and life may not be actively terminated by any human being, however noble their intentions.

Additionally, it should be noted that proponents of the Assisted Dying Bill claim that safeguards will protect the vulnerable. However, the UK Abortion Act 1967 may be used as a comparable example. It was intended, amongst other things, to protect unborn children, yet it has been totally disregarded and has led to anarchy with widespread abortion taking place outside of the Act. Morality has been negated and the ethic of the law ignored. So whilst the proponents of the Bill argue that there are safeguards in place which will protect people, probably in time these too will be ignored.

When it comes to appreciating the principles of halachah, Maimonides' words should be carefully considered. He writes:

"The law (halachah) does not take exceptional circumstances into account, it is not based on conditions which rarely occur. Whatever the law teaches, whether it be of an intellectual, moral or practical character, it is founded on what is the rule and not what is the exception; it ignores the injury that might be caused to a single person through a certain maxim or a certain Divine precept ... The laws cannot, like medicine, vary according to the different conditions of persons and times."[15]

Of course it is painful to see others suffering and it is for this reason that amongst the core Torah principles are that of compassion and helping our fellow man. The proponents of assisted dying and euthanasia deem their acts as 'mercy-killing' rather than murder. However, the term 'mercy-killing' cannot detract from the fact that such an act undermines the very principle that we do not own our own bodies and that purity of motive in terminating a life to relieve suffering does not make it acceptable.[16]

Notes

1. *Laws of Sanhedrin* end of ch. 18.
2. *Exodus* 20:13.
3. *Psikta Rabati* Parshah 25.
4. *Genesis* 9:5 see *Torah Temimah* ad loc. and *Minchat Chinuch* mitzvah 34.
5. Deuteronomy 25:3.
6. *Mishneh Torah, Laws of Injury and Damage* 5:1.
7. YD 236:2-3 and HM 420:31.
8. *Shulchan Aruch Ha'Rav* HM *The Laws of Damage to the Body and Soul* 4. See also *Responsa Igrot Moshe* YD 3:140, where Rabbi Feinstein rules that a person may not donate his body for experimentation after his death because his body is not his own to give away.
9. *Deuteronomy* 35:31.
10. *Mishneh Torah, Laws of Murder* 1:4.

11. *Laws of Sanhedrin* end of chapter 18, Radvaz says that the reason why a person may give testimony for his monetary aspects is because his money is his own, on the other hand, he may not give testimony that will make him face capital punishment because a person does not own his own body to cause himself harm.

12. *T. B. Yoma* 86a.

13. *Gesher Ha'Hayyim* (Jerusalem, 1960) chapter 25, quoted by Rosner *Medicine in The Bible and The Talmud* (Ktav, 1995) p. 283.

14. Rabbi Samson Raphael Hirsch, *Horeb*, translated by Dayan I Grunfeld, (NY: Soncino Press, 1997) p. 64.

15. *Moreh Nevuchim – Guide for the Perplexed,* III:34.

16. When facing the issue of assisted dying there has been much debate and discussion about refusing palliative care and prolonged treatment. This has been legalised in the form of Living Wills, whereby a person signs a declaration that they refuse certain treatments. It is beyond the scope of this work to explore all the issues here. However, there is a particular relevance to autonomy. This may be an area where autonomy and halachah meet. There may be circumstances where prolonged treatment does *not cure but prolongs the suffering of the patient.* In such a case, withholding of treatment may be up to the patient as long as certain conditions are met which, amongst other points, include the important fact of it being *passive* and not *active*. However, it must be emphasised that this does not contradict the clear distinction made above between autonomous secular ethics and heteronomous religious ethics, because here the area or aspect of autonomy is working *within* halachah and therefore part of heteronomous ethics, not autonomous ethics. The following articles are particularly useful here, Rav Yigal Bezalel Shafran, *Administering Medical Treatment to Parents Against Their Wishes, Crossroads Halacha and the Modern World,* (Zomet Institute Urim Publications, 1999), volume 5, pp. 65-89 and Professor Vardit Ravitsky, *Timers on Ventilators,* BMJ, volume 330, 19 February 2005, pp. 415-417. See also the final chapter of this book *Ventilators on Timers – Achievements in Israel.*

Part 3

The Doctor and the Patient

"I will neither give a deadly drug to anybody who asked for it, nor will I make a suggestion to this effect. Similarly, I will not give to a woman an abortive remedy. In purity and holiness I will guard my life and my art."

(Hippocratic Oath, 4th cent. B.C.E.)

Introduction

It would be murder if a third party acted to end a life, even if the person begged him to do so, and he believed that, in light of their great suffering, they would be better off dead. This is derived from a close examination of the verse, "The blood of your lives will I require; from the hand of every beast will I require it, and from the hand of man, from the hand of a person's brother, will I require the life of man."[1] What is the purpose of the final phrase, "from the hand of a person's brother, will I require the life of man"? A prohibition against fratricide would seem to follow logically from the prohibition against ordinary murder. According to Jewish Law, if a rule can be logically derived, there is no need for it to be explicitly stated in the Torah. Consequently, this verse must communicate some additional message. It may be argued that the apparent additional phrase is necessary to outlaw an act of killing even when the act is motivated by 'brotherly love,' i.e. by a misguided desire to mercifully end the life of a person suffering from excruciating pain.[2]

(Rabbi Yaakov Zvi Mecklenburg 1785-1865)

Imagine the scene.[3] A man comes into the synagogue one Shabbat morning and approaches the synagogue warden. He requests that Dr Goldberg be called up for an honour to the Torah.

The warden asks, "This is a most unusual request, why are you asking that Dr Goldberg be accorded an honour?"

"Well," replies the man, "You see, last night my father's illness deteriorated beyond all help, he was in terrible pain and all the family were gathered around his bed. We asked Dr Goldberg to help my father drink the barbiturates that would end his life. Dr Goldberg was fantastic, he held my father's hand, oh, he was so gentle with him, and helped him drink the concoction of drugs. The drugs did not quite take effect and my father was in great distress. Dr Goldberg gave him an injection to help Dad on his way. Dr Goldberg's compassion was beyond the call of duty. Please give him an honour this morning."

The warden, somewhat dazed at what he has heard, thinks that he should consult the rabbi. He walks to the rabbi's seat and tells him of the request. The rabbi turns white and says, "A man has committed such a sin of killing someone and the family request that he be given an honour. The answer is an emphatic no!"

The next day, Sunday, the synagogue council meet and a heated debate takes place concerning the rabbi's decision. Great concern is voiced that Dr Goldberg may leave the synagogue and take his supporters with him. The rabbi is not there to explain the halachic decision that he took and so people do not have the full picture.

The following Friday the headlines in *The Jewish Chronicle* newspaper read "Compassionate Doctor Banned from Synagogue." The article goes on to explain that the doctor was acting within the guidelines of the Government and Medical Association and that the doctor's father was a founder member of the synagogue. It also adds how Dr Goldberg is a patron of a cancer hospital for children and always has his patients' best interests at heart. Other local rabbis refuse to comment either on Dr Goldberg's actions or the rabbi's decision not to accord him an honour. Following the press coverage the synagogue board feels pressured to *deal with their rabbi*.

The following week *The Jewish Chronicle* newspaper prints a series of letters slamming the rabbi; the general thrust being that the rabbi is out of touch with the modern world as well as current medical opinion and legislation. One letter asks whether the rabbi had not learnt in school about the kindness of Abraham and asks therefore whether the rabbi lacks compassion as a result?

Any person who is familiar with our communities could see such a story reported in this way. But why wait for such a scenario to happen? Let us deal with this now and foresee a potential problem that may, God forbid, arise. The next section deals with doctors who kill and what would be the status of a doctor who administers a lethal injection. Moreover, it deals with how to view someone who has terminated their own life, for example, are they to be denied certain funeral rites?

Notes

1. *Genesis* 9:5.

2. *Ha'Ketav VeHa'Kabbalah.*

3. This depiction of events is fictitious but illustrative of a situation a rabbi could easily face in the future in the UK and indeed already in other countries where assisted dying and euthanasia have been legalised.

Chapter 8

The Best Doctors … [1]

> "One who is compassionate when they should be harsh (lit. cruel) will end up being harsh when they should be compassionate."
>
> (Midrash)[2]

On 7 September 1998, the medical world was rocked when the ghoulish activities of a particular general practitioner, Dr Harold Shipman, were exposed as mass murder. He was accused and convicted of killing 15 of his patients but it is believed that he may very well have killed at least 150 or more. Exact figures will never be known.[3]

The Book of Exodus is replete with civil laws.[4] The classic Biblical commentator Rashi (1040-1105), commenting on the verse which states "And these are the laws which you shall place before them …",[5] observes that the Hebrew letter "and" connects this passage to the events at Mt. Sinai, meaning just as the Ten Commandments were given at Sinai so were all the other laws.[6]

Amongst these passages that deal with civil law is the section that deals with a person who causes physical harm to another. The Torah says, "and he shall heal him."[7] One who causes injury to another must pay the medical bill. The Talmud explains that this provides a source that permits a doctor to heal a person, for had the Torah not allowed a doctor to heal, then the person who inflicted the injury would not have a medical bill to pay. As such, the doctor can, and indeed, must heal a person who is ill.[8]

The doctor-patient relationship is special, one in which the patient puts his trust. When that trust is abused, the relationship between doctor and patient is affected across the board, with the general public fearful of malpractice and incompetence. Doctors like Harold Shipman will have caused untold damage to the medical profession. Various recommendations and legislation have been drafted and implemented, so as to prevent a repeat of Dr Harold Shipman's evil escapade. But at the end of the day, however much governments legislate, evil cannot be totally eradicated. It is impossible to create laws for every single eventuality. We can of course try within reason, but in the end those who are thoroughly evil will deviously bypass the law through loopholes, and through their wicked schemes will still wreak havoc in the community.

The Mishnah states that "... the best doctors go to hell."[9] This is an alarming statement and one wonders whether this is to be understood literally or whether it is hyperbole. Maybe it is to be understood to refer to just a small proportion of doctors and thereby highlights the dangers that some doctors may face. Over the ages various explanations have been offered.

Rabbi Yom Tov Lipman Heller (1579-1654) explains the statement by suggesting that the doctor is not afraid of illness and so he indulges in good food; he does not instil humility in his heart towards the Almighty; furthermore, he sometimes kills people and when he has the capability to heal a poor man he refuses to do so.[10]

Rabbi Joseph Chayyim of Baghdad (1832-1909) explains that the doctor, who is not the best, but average, is cautious so as not to administer a wrong drug. The best doctors, however, will more than often take more chances and often risk a drug on a patient, which may, rather than cure them, make their condition worse and possibly even kill them.[11]

Rabbi Israel Lipschutz (1782-1860) explains the Mishnah as follows. It is related that when the Jewish People came out of Egypt, Moses' fame spread through the world. People and leaders marvelled at this great man who had led the Jewish People out of Egypt, which was the superpower in the world at that time. A certain king commissioned a portrait of Moses. He sent his finest artist to go and paint Moses in the desert. On the artist's return the king brought together his wise men and asked them (using an ancient and mystical art whereby looking at a person's face they could determine the character of a person) what they thought of Moses.

The wise men said that this was the face of a low-life person, a murderer and robber. Moreover, they claimed that the image represented someone who lacked decent qualities. The king was surprised at their verdict and accused his advisors of making a grave error, yet they insisted that they were right. When the king told his wise men that this was in fact a portrait of Moses, they were mortified. They retorted that clearly the artist had made an error. The artist however, stood his ground and counter-argued that the wise men had got it wrong.

The king decided to take the portrait and look at Moses himself to see if indeed the picture was accurate. When he reached the area where the Jewish people were encamped and he saw Moses he could not believe what he saw. The picture was accurate. How could it be though that it portrayed the face of a murderous low-life?

The king entered Moses' tent and prostrated himself before Moses. The king told Moses he was going to return to his city and sack his ignorant advisers. Moses told him not to for his advisers were correct. Moses explained that by nature he is no better than a dry piece of wood. He explained that he did in fact posses all of the aforementioned vices but that he had overcome them and tried to better himself.[12]

Rabbi Lipschutz explains that the meaning of the statement "… and the best doctors go to hell" refers to a person who *perceives* himself to be the best. For such a person would never consult medical books, nor ever consult colleagues. Moreover, he may administer medicines without properly ascertaining what harmful effects they may have on the patient. If the doctor pays no attention to these dangers then he is destined for hell. If, however, he learns from Moses' example and is aware that he is not better than anyone else, endeavours to improve himself and seeks to do the right thing then he will receive great reward.[13]

In summary, the consensus of scholars is that the statement "the best doctors go to hell" refers to specific situations of doctors who are either haughty, arrogant, or over-confident and, therefore, do not treat their patients effectively. It is a stark warning to all doctors to consult others and always to consider themselves as students of medicine who may continually learn from others.

I would add that this statement, "the best doctors go to hell" does not refer to the likes of Dr Harold Shipman, a cold-blooded and callous murderer. In the worst scenario, the Mishnah refers to a doctor whose intentions are essentially good but are misguided by complacency and lack of humility and so he relies solely on his own judgement. Shipman comes under a category far worse than what the rabbis were referring to because he wilfully murdered his victims. Perhaps there is a special place in hell for him.

We can learn from this Mishnaic statement the importance of a second opinion and that the two doctors should discuss their views together in order to find the best way to treat the patient. Humility is important for all of us to acquire and probably the most important attribute a doctor should possess. It follows, therefore, when discussing matters appertaining to life and death that it should take place within a religious context. But I think it goes further than this. I have laboured the point for some years in my own community that there needs to be a partnership between the patient, their family, the medical staff and the rabbi, and in some situations I have had success. I hope that the points raised in this book will help further this partnership.

Notes

1. This is largely based on a Shabbat morning address I gave in Leeds, 2000 (sidra Mishpatim, 5760) following the culmination of news about Dr Harold Shipman.

2. *Ecclesiastes Rabbah* 7:16. The Hozeh of Lublin quotes the Sages saying, "Whoever is compassionate where he should be cruel will eventually be cruel where he should be compassionate." He continued by saying that "a person needs to be master over all of his traits. If he fails to apply so-called negative traits in their proper times, he will end up applying them when it is wrong to do so. A person needs to know how to act in different circumstances, sometimes one way to further the will of Hashem and other times the exact opposite way for the same end." Rabbi Zelig Pliskin, *Growth Through Torah*, Parshat Toldot, pages 62-63, Aharon Yaakov Greenberg, *Torah Gems*, Parshat Toldot, p. 203.

3. In January 2001 a government report suggested that as many as 236 of Shipman's former patients may have been murdered. Further reports followed, none able to state conclusively the exact figure.

4. See especially chapters 21-24.

5. *Exodus* 21:1.

6. *Rashi* ad loc.

7. *Exodus* 21:19.

8. *T.B. Bava Kama* 85b.

9. *Mishnah Kiddushin* 4:14.

10. *Tosfot Yom Tov* ad loc.

11. *Ben Yehoyadah* ad loc.

12. The exact source of this story is unknown, moreover, it is not in all of the editions of the commentary *Tiferet Yisrael*. A similar story is quoted in *Shitah Mekubetzet, T. B. Nedarim* 32b paragraph *Shtei Anayim,* who quotes the story from the Re'aim but without naming Moses as the person in the story.

13. *Tiferet Yisrael, Mishnah Kiddushin* 4:14.

Chapter 9

Doctors who Administer Euthanasia[1]

"Rabbi Yochanan said, every Cohen who killed someone may not lift his hands [to duchan] as the verse states, 'your hands are full of blood'."

(Talmud)[2]

One of the more serious matters regarding assisted dying is how to view doctors who engage in this activity. Are they to be regarded as murderers, are they to be precluded from honours in the synagogue? May a doctor who is a Cohen duchan (bless the congregation) if he has been involved in this activity? The response to these matters will affect the doctor and the rabbi implementing the decision and will have wider implications for the community as a whole.

When we lived in ghettoed communities, the Beth Din (Jewish Court) was able to impose sanctions against people who breached halachah on a regular basis. This often took the form of ostracism from the community.[3] However, for more than two hundred years now, the ghetto walls have fallen and the Jewish people are able to integrate and, in some cases, have assimilated with their Gentile neighbours, so ostracism would be ineffective. Despite the fact that we no longer live in ghettoes, nevertheless, the majority of Jewish people tend to live close to one another and belong to a synagogue. This has enabled the communal feeling to continue to be fostered amongst most Jewish people. As such, although many Jews may have assimilated, nevertheless, for the majority the synagogue still remains largely the hub of communal life. What goes on there often has wider implications for other Jewish communal organisations and the community as a whole. Because of this cohesion through synagogue life, rabbis over the last few decades have explored what sanctions should be imposed against people who, for example, have married out of the faith and still attend the synagogue. Are they to be counted in a minyan or be given an honour in the synagogue? Similarly, rabbis have discussed how a husband who refuses to give his wife a bill of divorce should be dealt with. Is he to be shamed in the synagogue or denied synagogal honours? These questions have been addressed in the responsa of the eminent rabbis of our time and in practical terms, communities have established ways to react to these situations and indeed some of these rulings have been modified over the years.[4]

The Chief Rabbi Sir Jonathan Sacks has distilled the relevant lenient opinions on this matter in his book *One People*.[5] He explains that many eminent rabbis of the nineteenth and twentieth centuries were lenient in their considerations of those who, for example, transgress the Shabbat or other such cardinal mitzvot. Amongst them is Rabbi Yaakov Ettlinger (1798-1871), who was asked in 1861 whether someone who publicly desecrates the Shabbat is regarded as having placed himself outside the community and consequently whether his wine should be prohibited. Rabbi Ettlinger admits that he found it difficult to determine the status of a person who, on the one hand desecrates the Shabbat, yet on the other hand does make Kiddush at home and prays in the synagogue on Shabbat. In one way he denies Creation, yet in another way he acknowledges it.[6] He explains that such a person may not realise that their actions are prohibited and, as such, it is difficult to consider them *deliberate* sinners. They sin out of habit and cultural influence rather than from conviction. Moreover, their children are to be regarded more leniently still, for they are simply following the example of their parents.[7] So, they are sinners but not heretics and they remain within the halachic community. Rabbi Sacks quotes other eminent rabbis who concurred with this approach, including Rabbi Dovid Zvi Hoffman (1843-1921) who allowed such individuals to be included in a minyan for prayer.[8] Rabbi Yosef Shaul Nathansohn (1817-1878) agreed.[9] Rabbi Chayyim Ozer Grodzinski (1863-1940) included Rabbi Ettlinger's reasoning in his ruling that Shabbat desecrators might be counted in certain circumstances as valid witnesses.[10] Rabbi Avraham Yeshaya Karelitz (Chazon Ish 1878-1953)[11] and Rav Kook (1864-1935)[12] ruled that the category of heretic was inapplicable today.[13]

Whilst this approach has been accepted in many Orthodox communities, it would be wrong to assume that it should be applied in all circumstances. If, for example, an area of halachah, such as taking the life of another person, is regarded as clearly forbidden, how would Judaism view someone who regularly does this? Are they to be penalised? Is the community required to make a clear stand and to deny them synagogal honours to demonstrate quite clearly that such activity is not accepted by the Jewish community? Or are communities simply to adopt the stance that someone who takes the life of another means no harm and only wishes to relieve suffering?

It must be pointed out that not all halachic authorities share the leniency of Rabbi Ettlinger and those who followed his opinion. Some eminent halachic authorities have taken the view that, despite cultural changes in the set-up of Jewish communities, a Shabbat desecrator is still to be considered strictly and should be denied synagogal honours regardless of the occasion.[14] Amongst these are Rabbi Alexander Sender Shor (d. 1737),[15] Rabbi Chaim

Elazar Shapiro (1891-1936/7),[16] and Rabbi Hadiah (1895-1990),[17] who ruled that a Shabbat desecrator is considered like an idolater. Although these rabbis spoke of breaking Shabbat and idolatry,[18] it would appear that the sin of murder would be similarly viewed in a severe light.

So, how does Judaism in Modern times view a doctor who is wilfully involved in euthanasia? To suggest ostracism would be ineffective for the likelihood is that he would simply attend another synagogue elsewhere. We will now address the issues of synagogue honours and duchaning.

The halachah in the Shulchan Aruch is clear regarding a Cohen who *inadvertently* killed someone, that even if he repented he may not duchan.[19] Although Rabbi Moses Isserles (1530-1572) disagrees,[20] he would certainly agree when the Cohen *knowingly* killed someone that he may not duchan.[21] Moreover, our case of a doctor who willingly terminates someone's life is considered much worse, for he has willingly transgressed a capital offence and may be doing so on a regular basis. Moreover, Rav Glikman rules that a Cohen who performs abortions may not duchan,[22] so all the more it may be argued that a doctor who actively terminates someone's life may not duchan. Thus, the ruling on this matter should be clear that a doctor who is a Cohen and who performs euthanasia may not duchan.

Concerning honours in the synagogue, the following may be very useful reference points. Rabbi Moshe Feinstein (1895-1986) wrote a number of responsa considering giving honours to people who have deviated from halachah. His responses are measured and vary depending on the situation with which he was presented. For example, concerning someone who married out of the faith he permitted them to open the Aron Ha'Kodesh but not to be called-up.[23] On the other hand, for someone who is unobservant he did permit a call-up for a yahrtzeit but not at other times.[24] Further still, he precluded Reform rabbis from synagogue honours altogether.[25] Interestingly, Rabbi Feinstein forbade the honour of a call-up to a father who did not allow his son to have a circumcision but allowed the uncircumcised son to be called-up. This is based on the reasoning that the son is under his father's dominion and therefore not yet able to arrange his own circumcision.[26] Rabbi Feinstein did not have one rule for all, but a different response to different situations.

The case of a doctor who performs euthanasia should be considered far more severely than one who has married out of the faith. Communities who give a call-up (on a yahrtzeit) to someone who has married out do so because sadly the severity of intermarriage has become weakened in people's eyes, or the person's upbringing and cultural influences were not so strong in Jewish values. As a result, they may have married out due to a combination of circumstances rather than a formal rejection of Torah beliefs and values. It is for this reason that many communities are lenient and allow call-ups for a yahrtzeit. However, taking a life of another person, albeit to relieve suffering, is something that many consider to be wrong. To think otherwise undermines the very basis of human existence and the most fundamental principles of the Torah. It would be a weak argument to suggest that a doctor aims to relieve suffering and therefore does not consider his act as one of murder. If we are to accept the denial of the sanctity of life through an act of euthanasia then we lose all fundamental principles on which the Torah is based. It would appear therefore implausible that a doctor who is involved in euthanasia be given synagogal honours. For how can he hold the Torah scroll and recite the blessing when he transgresses the prohibition of "you shall not murder"?[27]

Notes

1. I have specifically addressed the issue of doctors who administer euthanasia, rather than doctors involved in assisted dying who 'merely' pass the patient the barbiturates, because the latter case appears more complex to define in relation to being denied synagogal

honours. This is because the doctor does not actively administer the drugs, he 'merely' passes them to the patient. However, it should not be inferred that they might be honoured; this will be for leading halachic authorities to decide.

2. *Isaiah* 1:15, *T. B. Brachot* 32b.

3. *Shulchan Aruch* YD 334.

4. For example, when I was the Rav in Cardiff United Synagogue (1993-1999), there was a long–standing edict by the late and much revered Rav Rogosnitsky who did not allow any Reform Jew to have an honour in the synagogue. The Chief Rabbi Sir Jonathan Sacks and his Beth Din subsequently rescinded this ruling in a lengthy responsum. In a copy of the ruling which I possess, the Chief Rabbi explained that whilst the edict may have been effective years ago, today however, membership of Reform in itself is not a reason to be precluded from being given an honour. The Chief Rabbi's ruling was subsequently implemented in the synagogue. Of course, this only applies to those who are halachically Jewish.

5. For a full appreciation of the points made by Rabbi Sacks it is worth reading the full analysis and reasoning in *One People,* chapter six.

6. *Rashi T. B. Chullin* 5a elucidates that the reason why a Shabbat desecrator is considered like an idolater is because he denies Creation. As such, one who doesn't fully observe i.e. breaks Shabbat in some respects yet observes other aspects, falls into a peculiar category.

7. *Responsa Binyan Tziyon Hachadashot* 23. See also *Responsa Igrot Moshe* OH 1:33 where he clarifies the difference between one who desecrates the Shabbat in private in contrast to one who desecrates the Shabbat in public and how he explains the situation today.

8. *Responsa Melamed Lehoil* 1:29.

9. *Responsa Shoel Umeshiv* cited ibid.

10. *Responsa Achiezer* 3:25. See also *Achiezer* 4:3.

11. *Chazon Ish* YD 2:16. However, it should be noted that not all agree in their understanding of the Chazon Ish. Rabbi Yitzchak Yosef quotes those who are of the opinion that since the Chazon Ish specified later in the same section (YD 2:28) that he was referring to those who have not been shown the error of their ways and have not been rebuked, it stands to reason that where a person has been informed of the severity of Shabbat and continues to desecrate it, he may not be viewed in a lenient fashion *Yalkut Yosef, Laws of Honouring Parents,* volume 2 p. 23.

12. *Igeret Harayah* 1:138.

13. Chief Rabbi Sir Jonathan Sacks, *One People*, pp. 118-121. See also Rabbi Yaakov Kamenetsky (1891-1986), who rules that relatives of people who have died who desecrated Shabbat, must observe all mourning laws. He makes three points to support this: 1) they do not realise the severity of Shabbat, 2) even if they studied a little in their youth, it is insufficient to engrain in them the *severity* of the prohibition and 3) even if they see other observant Jews and have religious relatives they consider them "peculiar" [and therefore they do not make a positive impact on them], *Emet Le'Yaakov on Four Volumes of Tur and Shulchan Aruch*, (NY: Rabbi Jacob Joseph School Press, 2000), p. 393 footnote 218.

14. Rabbi Yitzchak Yosef makes a distinction between the case of Rabbi Ettlinger where the person still has some recognition of Shabbat, in contrast to someone who does not pray in the synagogue on Shabbat and does not recite Kiddush, because the latter may be considered a *mumar* (heretic). However, he suggests other possible reasons to be lenient. See *Yalkut Yosef, Laws of Honouring Parents*, volume 2 pp. 21-25.

15. *Simlah Chadashah* YD 2:16.

16. *Responsa Minchat Elazar* 1:74.

17. *Responsa Yaskil Avdi* 8:19.

18. Maimonides *Mishneh Torah, Laws of Shabbat* ch. 30 groups together Shabbat and idolatry because they go to the very essence of belief. However, in various places the Talmud groups together idolatry, sexual immorality and murder because they are considered three cardinal sins, for which a person should be willing to sacrifice his life rather than transgress.

19. *Shulchan Aruch* OH 128:35, the reason for this is that the hands that spilled blood may not function now as a vehicle for a blessing, see *Mishneh Berurah* ad loc.

20. *Shulchan Aruch* ad loc.

21. See *T. B. Brachot* 32a and so it may be clearly inferred from Rabbi Isserles.

22. *Noam* (5738) volume 20, p. 171 Quoted by Professor Steinberg *Encyclopaedia Hilchatit Refuit*, volume 2, *Hapalah* p. 102. Halachists have discussed the law regarding a doctor who inadvertently kills someone, would he in Temple times have to go into exile to the "Cities of Refuge,"? *Birkei Yosef* YD 336:6, *Yad Avraham* ad loc. See also *Shulchan Shlomoh*, volume 1, pp. 132-3. Our discussion is far more serious for the doctor *willingly* kills.

23. *Responsa Igrot Moshe* OH 2:51. In 1945 (Rosh Chodesh Nissan 5705) Chief Rabbi Hertz and the London Beth Din (Dayan Lazarus, Dayan Abramsky and Dayan Grunfeld) issued a letter forbidding people who have married out from joining a synagogue. They did rule, however, that if the person was already a member before they married out that they may continue their membership but not hold office. This rule still applies in many communities today.

24. *Responsa Igrot Moshe* OH 3:21.

25. *Responsa Igrot Moshe* OH 3:21; moreover, he forbids answering *Amen* after their brachah.

26. *Responsa Igrot Moshe* OH 2:33 p.217.

27. Perhaps he could be given an honour such as opening the Aron Ha'Kodesh when he has yahrtzeit, although this too may be questionable. Ultimately, the practical response to these questions will be for the leading halachic authorities to decide upon.

Chapter 10

Sound Mind

"The general rule of the matter concerning one who wilfully takes their own life is that we consider extenuating circumstances[1] of any sort, such as [the person is] afraid, in pain, or mentally deranged or the person thinks that it is a mitzvah to terminate their life to avoid sin, and matters similar to these. This is because it is an unlikely thing that a person would commit such a despicable act [of wilful suicide] with a clear mind."

(Rabbi Y. M. Epstein 1829-1907)[2]

The sages described a *wilful suicide* as follows:

"Who is to be counted as a suicide? Not one who climbs to the top of a tree or to the top of a roof, and falls to his death. Rather it is one who says, 'Behold, I am going to climb to the top of the tree, or to the top of the roof, and then throw myself down to my death.' And thereupon, others see him climb to the top of the tree, or to the top of the roof and fall to his death. Such an act is presumed to be a suicide, and for such a person no rites whatsoever should be observed."[3]

There are discrepancies in the text above and these variations make a difference in defining the precise preconditions required to qualify as a wilful suicide. Rabbi Sidney Goldstein has explored the various halachic interpretations in his comprehensive book *Suicide In Rabbinic Literature* and they need not be reiterated here.[4] What is relevant in practice is how this law manifests in the Shulchan Aruch. Rabbi Yosef Caro (1488-1575) crystallises the halachic approach:

> "What is considered a *wilful suicide*? For example, *he said* he is going up to the top of the roof, and *they saw* that he went up *immediately* in an *angry way*, or he was *distressed* and fell and died, this is one who has wilfully ended his life. But if they saw him strangled and hanging from a tree or slain and lying on his sword he has the status of a regular dead person."[5]

According to the Shulchan Aruch, the following conditions must be in place:

1. He must make a declaration of intent before his death.
2. The act must be followed immediately with his proposed actions.
3. He must be in an angry or distressed state.
4. There must be witnesses.[6]

If any of these conditions is missing it appears that the Shulchan Aruch would not consider the death as a *wilful suicide*.

Halachah has always had room for compassion concerning suicide. Because of this, rabbis over the years, when faced with tragic circumstances (of a family discovering a dead relative or friend), decided that unless there was concrete evidence as fleshed out above in the

Shulchan Aruch, an appropriate stance was taken and the person was not assumed to be a *wilful suicide*. Of course in an occurrence of a *wilful suicide* the halachah denied various mourning rites and eulogies[7] and in some cases buried the person in another part of the cemetery.

When I was Rav in Cardiff, I was called to perform a funeral in a cemetery in Brynmawr, Gwent, a small Welsh Valley community. The deceased was the last living Jewess in the village. At the turn of the twentieth century there had been some twenty Jewish communities sprawled across Wales. I arrived at the cemetery, which had no more than maybe a few hundred Jewish graves – there was still ample open space in the cemetery that will never be used. To the right of the cemetery gates, and at a considerable distance from the rest of the graves, was a lonely grave of a lady buried in the 1960s. I enquired from some of the people there as to why she had been buried so far from all the other graves and they told me that sadly she had committed suicide. Because of this she was not buried in the cemetery together with the rest of the community. I felt sorry for her. First because of her tragic demise and secondly, because she had been banished and singled out so publicly. As well as the ruling of the Shulchan Aruch, I was reminded of the ruling of Rabbi Epstein, who spells out so clearly room for leniency with a suicide victim. He writes:

"The general rule of the matter concerning one who wilfully takes their own life is, that we consider extenuating circumstances of any sort, such as [the person is] afraid, in pain, or mentally deranged or the person thinks that it is a mitzvah to terminate their life to avoid sin, and matters similar to these. This is because it is an unlikely thing that a person would commit such a despicable act [of wilful suicide] with a clear mind."[8]

Rabbi Epstein provides the clearest guidelines to allow for manoeuvrability in these tragic circumstances. I wondered whether this poor girl should have been considered more compassionately. That is, unless there is clear evidence that a person was of sound mind and willingly took their life, they are assumed to be of unsound mind or in Freudian terms psychologically unbalanced and therefore not to be treated as a suicide.[9]

Lord Joffe's proposed Dying Bill requires mental competence as a precondition to assisted dying and euthanasia. Indeed the Bill proposes that a document must be signed before the death can take place. The same is true in countries where this is the law. However, from a halachic perspective, there may be instances when a person signed a document consenting to euthanasia or assisted dying many months or even years prior to it actually taking place. As such, they may not be considered a *wilful suicide* because their statement is not followed immediately by suicide. Moreover, at the point of death they may no longer be of sound mind due to fear and the severely distressing pain that they now experience. The stark consequence of this may be that the doctor who engages in euthanasia is treated more severely than some people who undergo euthanasia. This is because, in certain circumstances, the patient may be considered of unsound mind and therefore an *un-wilful suicide*, and as such, they should be treated as a normal death with full funeral rites. On the other hand, the doctor who administers euthanasia (and who is definitely of sound mind) will always be considered as having transgressed a serious sin.

Notes

1. The Hebrew is "teliyah" lit. something to hang on to.
2. *Aruch Ha'Shulchan* (circa 1890) YD 345:5.
3. *Mes. Semachot* 2:2.
4. Sidney Goldstein, *Suicide in Rabbinic Literature*, (NY: Ktav, 1989).

5. *Shulchan Aruch* YD 345:1-3.

6. For a further leniency see *S'dei Chemed,* Rabbi Medini, volume 5, pp. 54-55, who quotes various opinions that say unless a person was *warned* by witnesses and told of the severity of the sin and despite that took their own life, they are not considered a *wilful suicide*.

7. *Shulchan Aruch* YD 345:1.

8. *Aruch Ha'Shulchan* (circa 1890) YD 345:5.

9. In fact some insurance companies in the last 15-20 years have decided to pay out for death on suicide since it is considered an *illness*.

Chapter 11

The Risk of Moral Bankruptcy

"If we are silent on key issues we risk a moral bankruptcy."[1]

There is a well known Jewish joke that goes as follows:

A guest rabbi visited a community and the synagogue beadle asked him what he was going to talk about.

"The sanctity of the family and married life," replied the rabbi.

"Oh, you'd better avoid that. We have a prominent member of the synagogue who recently was caught committing adultery: best leave that out," said the beadle.

"Then I will talk about Shabbat observance," said the rabbi.

"Oh don't talk about that, our wealthiest benefactor has to have his business running on the *Sabbath*, we do not want to upset him," advised the beadle.

"Don't worry, I will speak about theft and robbery," said the rabbi smiling.

"Oh no! We have a member who was recently imprisoned for fraud and his family will get upset," said the beadle.

The rabbi, feeling anxious said, "I cannot speak

about family, Shabbat or robbery, so what *can* I speak about?"

"Oh don't worry rabbi, just speak about Yiddishkeit!" exclaimed the beadle.

This is of course a joke. Indeed it is not uncommon for rabbis making guest appearances in synagogues to break the ice with this joke. In truth, it is more real than people would believe. Many rabbis have been advised to avoid a range of issues in case someone in the audience is offended. This is lamentable, since it prevents rabbis from dealing with key contemporary topics, for fear that someone may feel marginalised or upset.

I have often heard people say that, "Some rabbis are known as controversial whilst others are not." I believe that this misrepresents rabbis. I doubt that any rabbi seeks to be controversial for the sake of it, rather, they feel it necessary to speak out on certain key issues that they feel are pertinent at a particular point in time. Whether it is to do with speaking about matters connected with appropriate fundraising for charitable organisations, sexual morality, racism, Israel and non-Orthodoxy, to name just a few issues. I would prefer to say that there are rabbis who speak out and rabbis who do not. Why this is the case is not the purpose of this book: what is a point of focus however, is that if rabbis do not highlight and educate their communities and where possible, the wider community, we face a potential moral bankruptcy. Are ministers of religion simply to focus on issues that do not grate or make people uneasy or are they to guide and educate on a wide range of issues?

In order to address this, communal lay leaders and synagogue members must revise their perception of the functionary role of the rabbi. It is true that the rabbi does have an important role at life cycle events and he is also a teacher, but he is a guide as well. As such, members must observe the wider-ranging message of ministers whether it is from a short address from the pulpit or a more lengthy discourse.

Of course sensitivity must be shown and messages packaged in digestible morsels that will ultimately enable people to appreciate the Torah message. But key issues cannot and must not be avoided altogether. If rabbis are afraid to talk about certain key moral, ethical, spiritual and religious matters they may face the risk of moral bankruptcy – not a direct moral bankruptcy, but an indirect moral bankruptcy – for they may very well diminish themselves and the Torah values they stand for. The potential impact on communities could be vast. Alternatively, the rabbi has a huge opportunity and, if he addresses key issues in an appropriate manner, he may succeed in making vital changes to the way people think and may enrich their lives spiritually.

Note

1. See also D. Prager and J. Telushkin, "You do not have to do something bad in order to do bad: you only have to do nothing," *The Nine Questions People Ask About Judaism*, (NY: Simon and Schuster, 1981) p. 43.

Chapter 12

Speak Out for the Unborn Child[1]

On 24 October 2006, in Miami, Florida at the Baptist Children's Hospital, a 'tiny tot' stunned doctors by surviving being born at just 21 weeks and 6 days. Amillia Taylor was no longer than a fountain pen and weighed just 10 ounces. She is thought to be the first baby known to survive after a gestation period of fewer than 23 weeks. Amillia did experience respiratory problems, a very mild brain haemorrhage and some digestive problems, but none of the health concerns is expected to pose long-term problems. Amillia was placed in an incubator after her birth and after a few months was able to go home. She was conceived by in-vitro-fertilisation and delivered by Caesarean section. Amillia is Sonja and husband Eddie's first child.

Liberal attitudes suffered a recent setback when the Assisted Dying Bill, which would have taken us a step down the road to euthanasia, was defeated in the House of Lords. Perhaps the pendulum may be swinging against the permissive approach to abortions. Certainly, in the United States, there has been a marked shift to the right.

In February 2006, lawmakers in South Dakota approved the most far-reaching ban on abortion yet in an American state. According to the new law, passed by the South

Dakota Senate by 23 votes to 12, it is a felony for doctors to perform any abortion, except to save the life of a pregnant woman. Similar measures have been introduced in Ohio, Indiana, Georgia, Tennessee, and Kentucky. This sets the stage for new legal challenges that will seek to reverse the Supreme Court's historic ruling in Roe v. Wade from 1973, which recognised the right of a woman to terminate her pregnancy.[2]

In addition, it must be noted that the period of viability that is discussed by doctors from a secular perspective, was thrown in turmoil when on 24 October 2006 Amillia Taylor was born after 21 weeks and 6 days and weighed just 10 ounces. She is thought to be the first baby known to survive after a gestation period of fewer than 23 weeks. Doctors and the public should be mindful of this.

Across the world more than 44 million abortions take place every year, the equivalent of 120,000 abortions per day. In England and Wales, 190,000 abortions are recorded annually. I doubt that those who sponsored the UK Abortion Act 1967 envisaged such astounding statistics.

In Britain especially, it is clear that abortion has become a widely used form of contraception. In 2003, Joanna Jepson, a Church of England curate, challenged the legality of the abortion of a 24 week-old foetus with a cleft palate. When I spoke about this in the synagogue, it was greeted by some of my congregation with clear discomfort. "Shabbat morning is not the time to discuss these matters," I was told.

When is the right time? People are reluctant to attend midweek talks on such topics. It is a peculiar anomaly in our society that pro-life campaigners are less outspoken than, say, animal-rights activists.

Trends in the West are often set in America and gradually filter across the Atlantic. Just as American finance influences the UK economy, so too, the moral and religious climate in the UK is affected by what happens overseas. Traditionally, change may take place more slowly in the UK, but eventually it does occur.[3] In early 2006, the Chief Rabbi Sir Jonathan Sacks wrote a letter of support to the Right to Life Charitable Trust, the educational charity linked to the anti-abortion campaign group Right to Life. One of its trustees is the Jewish philanthropist Godfrey Bradman. The Chief Rabbi gave his personal backing to the group's efforts to ensure that "the message of the sanctity of human life be conveyed as widely as possible." It was a positive move, and more work is still needed. Pulpit rabbis are often inclined to shy away from what appear to be contentious issues for fear of rocking the boat. Judaism, however, by its very nature, has something to say on the critical issues that affect us, especially those pertaining to life and death.

Should we stand back and let Catholic or Muslim communities lead the way while we wait in the shadows, or are Jewish communities ready to be "a light unto the nations?"[4]

Israel – whose severely high rate of abortion has cost it more than one million children[5] in the last 60 years or so – has begun to make some progress both in educating parents and lowering the rate of abortion. Most significantly is Friends of Efrat, a group of volunteers who identify strongly with the goal that no Jewish child should be lost to the Jewish people because of the economic worries of the parents. No Jewish woman should have to go through an abortion owing to financial anxieties. Just $1,000 (around £500) saves one life; over the past 30 years, more than 20,000 lives have been saved – often to the parents' delight.[6]

Jewish communities here are affected by abortion and it won't go away simply by not talking about it. Hopefully, the sea-change in the USA will prick the conscience of other Westerners. Interestingly, this now seems to be happening. In April 2007, the *Independent* reported a crisis because an unprecedented number of doctors are now refusing to perform abortions. Jeremy Laurance reported the following:

"Distaste at performing terminations combined with ethical and religious convictions has led to a big increase in 'conscientious objectors' who request exemption from the task, the Royal College of Obstetricians and Gynaecologists (RCOG) says. A key factor is what specialists call 'the dinner party test.' Gynaecologists who specialise in fertility treatment creating babies for childless couples are almost universally revered – but no one boasts of being an abortionist. As a result, after decades of campaigning, anti-abortion organisations may be on the point of achieving their objective by default. Repeated efforts to tighten the law have failed and public opinion remains firmly in support, but the growing number of doctors refusing to do the work means there may soon not be enough prepared to carry out terminations to meet demand."[7]

By and large there has been a deafening silence in the Jewish community. This must now change. Rabbis and educated lay leaders should perhaps consider creating a suitable partnership with pro-life campaigners, as well as running seminars to highlight the Jewish view of abortion. Most importantly, they should foster a relationship with doctors in their community so that they understand the relevant medical-halachic issues. Abortion could also form a crucial topic for interfaith dialogue.

I am sure that couples do not consider an abortion lightly. It is a highly sensitive subject. But that does not mean running away from it. Rabbis should take the lead in publicly addressing the issues – and also ensure that the right counselling support is available for those who need it.

* * *

Animal rights, abortion and euthanasia are three crucial issues of our time. They are all important and all worthy of lengthy discussions in their own right. Similarly passive smoking is an important issue amongst others. But society, even governments and certainly religious groups, have an obligation to ensure that there is a sense of proportion and priority in knowing which issues to address first and which to devote the most time discussing. I hope that you, the reader, will have learned something from this short book and that you will feel a desire to learn more about some of the topics herein. Perhaps it will mean purchasing another book of Jewish interest or maybe it will give you the impetus to attend an adult education group. If you are a medical professional, see if you can create a partnership with your rabbi and together delve further into some of the pertinent matters we have raised. If you do decide to act then I know I will have succeeded and, more importantly, so will you.

Notes

1. This chapter was first published in *The Jewish Chronicle*, 16 June 2006. I was deeply honoured to see that Friends of Efrat had posted this article on their website www.efrat.org.il; it has been published here with some changes.

2. However, it should be noted that in November 2006 South Dakota held a referendum on the matter, and the ban on abortion passed by the legislature was overturned by the electorate. Nevertheless, the earlier ruling does show that some people are beginning to be more vocal in their objections to the abortion laws and other States may yet be successful in implementing changes to the law. Moreover, lawmakers in South Dakota are likely to modify the law for reconsideration, this time to include exceptions for abortion for rape and incest as well as the previous exception to save the life of the pregnant mother.

3. Indeed in October 2007 when I was preparing the final draft of this book some MPs were calling for the limit for abortion in the UK to be lowered from 24 weeks to 20 weeks. The debate coincided with the fortieth anniversary of the UK Abortion Act 1967.

4. *Isaiah* 42:6.

5. Friends of Efrat estimate that there may be close to 50,000 abortions each year in Israel.

6. The figure to date is of course now much higher.

7. Jeremy Laurance, Health Editor, *Abortion crisis as doctors refuse to perform surgery, The Independent,* 16 April 2007, http://news. independent.co.uk/uk/health_medical/article2452408.ece.

Epilogue

1

Infanticide in Ancient Egypt and Abortion in Modern Times[1]

"Facing a fate we cannot change, we are called upon to make the best of it rising above ourselves and growing beyond ourselves, in a word, by changing ourselves. And this equally holds for the three components of the 'tragic triad' – pain, guilt, and death – inasmuch as we may turn suffering into a human achievement and accomplishment; derive from guilt the opportunity to change for the better; and see in life's transitoriness an incentive to take responsible action."

(Viktor Frankl 1905-1997)[2]

We say in the Haggadah, "Go and learn what Laban the Syrian tried to do to our father Jacob. While Pharaoh decreed only against the newborn males, Laban tried to uproot all of Israel."

Pharaoh decreed that every newly-born male be killed at birth.[3] This was nothing short of a decree of infanticide; mass murder of Jewish male children. Indeed Pharaoh's rule was set against the Egyptian male babies as well.[4] Like the Nazis who enshrined their evil in law, so too here, the decree of the king was the law.

In order to ensure that his decree was executed appropriately he appointed two midwives called Shifrah and Puah to ensure that the children were killed. Nehama Leibowitz (1905-1997) describes two ancient traditions regarding who the midwives were. According to one tradition, they were Jews, Yocheved and Miriam.[5] Rashi explains that they were called Shifrah and Puah because Shifrah means to beautify the newborn child and Puah means to coo the baby who is crying in order to soothe it.[6]

According to the other tradition they were Egyptians.[7] The latter tradition is especially interesting because it transforms the story into an important philosophical text emphasizing the confrontation between an individual (Egyptian) and her own, rather than a foreign, government. Leibowitz sums up her study of the midwives with these words:

> "According to this interpretation, we must consider that the Torah shows us how, in a sea of evil and tyranny – and just after verse [Exodus] 1:13, which shows Egypt (the kingdom and the people) in their wickedness – an individual can stand up against evil, oppose an order, disobey it, and not shrug off his moral responsibility under cover of 'superior orders.' The Torah contrasts the brutal decrees of enslavement and massacre initiated by Pharaoh and supported by government and the people with the God-fearing 'civil disobedience' of the midwives."[8]

Not only did the midwives risk their own lives by allowing the children to be born and remain alive, but they went beyond the call of duty and provided food as well. No doubt if they had been found out by Pharaoh's guards, their fate would have been worse than death. As such, it comes as no surprise that Hashem rewarded them with the houses of the Cohanim, Levi'im and Kingship.[9]

In the classic work *Tomer Devorah* by Rabbi Moshe Cordovero (Ramak 1522-1570)[10] he explains that there are eight examples of kindness. The first is to look after children when born and to provide for their needs.[11]

Perhaps, therefore, it was for this reason that Shifrah and Puah didn't simply allow the children to live in a passive sense but proactively kept them alive; they beautified the babies, cooed and nourished them. This is the starting point of chessed – kindness. True kindness in Jewish thought is not simply not committing infanticide – that is "turning away from evil;" in Jewish thought, caring for, feeding and nourishing babies – is "pursuing good."[12]

The Midrash tells us more about Miriam. When Pharaoh first made his decree, her parents divorced, so as not to have any more children lest they have a son who would be killed. Miriam said to her parents, "Your decree is harsher than Pharaoh's, for he only decreed death to the boys, but by separating you are decreeing [death] to the boys and the girls." Miriam's parents Amram and Yocheved heeded the reprimand of their young daughter and re-married. From that union Moses was born.[13]

Miriam cared for the child before it was conceived and after it was born and no doubt ensured that it was looked after during the interim period whilst in the womb.

Shifrah and Puah turned a potential "tragic triad" of pain, guilt and death into a positive experience. With pain, they risked the possibility of Pharaoh inflicting them with pain should he have caught them disobeying his commands. They avoided the guilt of transgressing infanticide: and with death, they distanced themselves from death by saving the lives of the children. They saw in life's transitoriness an incentive to take responsible action.

The challenge that lies ahead of us all is to take challenging and difficult experiences and turn them into meaningful ones, precisely what Shifrah and Puah did. In some cases it is the prevention of death, in other instances it is following tragedy that meaning may be found. Viktor Frankl quotes the following moving story:

"A few years after World War II a doctor examined a Jewish woman who wore a bracelet made of baby teeth mounted in gold. 'A beautiful bracelet,' the doctor remarked. 'Yes,' the woman answered, 'this tooth belonged to Miriam, this one to Esther, and this one to Samuel ...' She mentioned the names of her daughters and sons according to age. 'Nine children,' she added, 'and all of them were taken to the gas chambers.' Shocked, the doctor asked: 'How can you live with such a bracelet?' Quietly, the Jewish woman replied: 'I am now in charge of an orphanage in Israel.'"

Frankl adds, "As you see, meaning may be squeezed out even from suffering, and that is the very reason why life remains potentially meaningful in spite of everything."[14]

I am reminded of the story in the Talmud about Rabbi Yochanan who would comfort mourners by showing them the tooth of his tenth child who had died.[15] I have often understood this piece of Talmud as Rabbi Yochanan displaying (idiosyncratic) empathy to others, but now wonder whether Rabbi Yochanan was showing people that meaning can still be found in life despite tragedy; after all, he was one of the greatest rabbis mentioned in the Talmud and achieved so much despite his own personal suffering.

It is astonishing the lengths some people go to in the name of nouveau intellectualism in their attempts to show the role of valiant women in the Tenach. We need look no further than the above passage about Shifrah and Puah – it is the most daring yet in the Torah and hard to match, for whereas most people receive a medal for one act of bravery, these women performed thousands of chivalrous acts.

In light of the discussion above, I now turn my attention to the subject of abortion in our time. There are ethicists who not only advocate abortion in practice but also justify, in theory at least, the concept of infanticide. Indeed British philosophers, most notably David Hume, Jeremy Bentham and John Stuart Mill, challenged the religious basis of morality and the absolute prohibition of suicide, euthanasia and infanticide. Whilst generally speaking Judaism mandates abortion when the life of the mother is at risk – which is indeed a rare phenomenon – it does not sanction abortion in the way society has allowed it to happen today. Rabbi Eliyahu Mizrachi (1455-1525/6) described abortion as "a capital crime without capital punishment." He meant that although capital punishment is not exacted against a Jew who commits an abortion, nevertheless, in its severity it is comparable to a capital offence.

The statistics for abortion make disturbing reading. Globally there are more than 44 million abortions conducted each year which equates to some 120,000 abortions each day. These figures eclipse the numbers of those who died in the trenches in WWI on a daily basis and those murdered in the Holocaust. In England and Wales, there are approximately 190,000 abortions per annum. And perhaps most importantly to us as a Jewish people, in Israel in 2005 there were 143,913 births and 19,928 abortions.[16] This means that approximately 20,000 abortions are performed each year in Israel.[17] I am reminded of the seemingly harsh statement in the Mishnah "The best doctors go to hell."[18] Many interpretations are given but we cannot escape a very literal meaning here in relation to doctors who perform abortions in cases where halachah forbids them. Yes they may be perceived as 'good' doctors in doing what society perceives to be 'right' or 'in the best interests of the mother' but if it does not conform with the Torah view then seemingly good acts may sometimes be considered barbarous acts.

The author of the Haggadah writes, "Pharaoh attempted to uproot the males but Laban wished to destroy all." Abortion in our times does not discriminate against boy or girl. It destroys everything in its path.

I feel that the subject of abortion is one that we do not face up to in the Jewish community and one from which religious leaders sometimes shy away as they see it as a controversial or sensitive issue. Yet this should not be the case.

In 2005 Pope John Paul II died. He was someone who continued to advocate a strong Catholic position, maintaining the strict prohibition on abortion[19] as well as a strong religious view concerning same sex marriages and other moral issues, yet he was still highly respected by many as a religious leader.

Passover is a time for asking questions. There is no more a challenging a form of question than introspection and asking ourselves, do we, God forbid, sometimes respect the views of other religions yet are intolerant of our own? As such, it behoves us as religious and moral beings to explore the Torah view on medical issues and to be proud of our Heritage. We should learn from the examples of Shifrah and Puah who realised the sanctity of life, and the other valiant women of that time who risked their own lives to do what was right. Our Sages said about them, "due to the reward of the righteous women in that generation, the Jewish people were redeemed from Egypt."[20]

Notes

1. This chapter is from my commentary on the Haggadah called *Matzah Ashirah* due to its relevance here.

2. V. Frankl, *Man's Search for Ultimate Meaning*, (NY: Basic Books, 2000), p. 142.

3. *Exodus* 1:16.

4. *Exodus* 1:22.

5. See *Rashi, Ibn Ezra, Rashbam and Ramban*, based on *T. B. Sotah* 11b.

6. *Rashi Exodus* 1:15.

7. See *Philo, Josephus, Midrash Tadshe, Abrabanel, Kli Yakar and Rabbi M. H. Luzzatto*.

8. *New Studies in Sefer Shmot,* (Jerusalem: World Zionist Organization, 1986), pp. 34-36.

9. *Rashi Exodus* 1:21.

10. Ramak was the teacher of the Arizal – Rabbi Isaac Luria (1534-1572).

11. *Tomer Devorah* chapter 5.

12. *Psalms* 34:15.

13. *Rashi Exodus* 2:1.

14. Frankl p. 142.

15. *T. B. Berachot* 5b.

16. Historical Abortion Statistics, Israel, compiled by Wm. Robert Johnston, www.johnstonsarchive.net/policy/abortion/ab-israel.html.

17. Some project an even higher figure.

18. *Kiddushin* 4:14.

19. Incidentally this is not quite the same as the Jewish view.

20. *T. B. Sotah* 11b.

2

Ventilators on Timers – Achievements in Israel

I present this final chapter cautiously. Throughout this book I have attempted to avoid practical aspects of halachah appertaining to the medical treatment of a dying person. However, since ventilators on timers have recently been installed in Israel and illustrate very poignantly how halachah and medicine may interface successfully, it therefore warrants some mention here. The subject is immense and I only provide an introduction to what is essentially a broad and complex subject. I further emphasise that before any practical steps are taken in this area, advice should be sought from a competent rabbi who is both knowledgeable in the relevant areas of halachah and who also has a full understanding of medical procedures, thereby being well equipped to give a Torah view of how to proceed in these matters.

It should not be assumed that because Judaism forbids any form of *active euthanasia* a person should continue with *prolonged suffering*. Rabbi Moshe Feinstein made a clear distinction between the concept of prolonging life and prolonging suffering. He explained that there may be certain circumstances in which it is within a person's choice whether or not they decide to be treated, where the treatment will not cure them but will keep them alive only to endure intolerable pain and anguish.[1] It cannot be emphasised enough that each patient's case must be assessed individually and that comparisons should not be made between cases without careful deliberation of the medical situation and halachic response to it. It is also interesting to note that a number of great rabbis, amongst them Rabbeinu Nissim (1310-1380), were of the opinion that a person may pray to die rather than suffer unbearable illness.[2]

There has been much discussion about the withdrawal and withholding of foods, fluids, oxygen, CPR and medications, and it is beyond the scope of this chapter to deal with these issues.[3] However, the matter of ventilators on timers, for reasons set out above, is something that needs some attention here.

In 2000, the Israeli Government set up a committee to explore the rights of the terminally ill. The Committee was named after its head, the renowned Professor Avraham Steinberg, an Orthodox rabbi, paediatric neurologist and medical ethicist. The 59-member public committee comprised physicians, scientists, medical ethicists, social workers, philosophers, nurses, lawyers, judges and clergymen representing the main religions in Israel.

On 15 December 2006, after years of preparation and a year after it was approved by the Knesset, The Terminally Ill Patients' Law 2005 came into effect. This law allows people to submit forms to the Health Ministry declaring how they would like to be treated if they become terminally ill.[4] These forms are stored on a computerised national register, accessible by all health funds and hospitals. The patient may also specify that they do not want to be placed on a respirator. The legislation was described by the then health-minister Dan Naveh as "on the human level, one of the most complicated and most important ever legislated by the Knesset. It is a great moral achievement for the dying and their families."[5]

It must be emphasised that the new law in Israel relates

only to a patient suffering from an incurable medical problem whose life expectancy, even if he is given medical treatment, does not exceed six months. The law also relates specifically to the terminally ill patient at the final stages of his life, i.e. when a number of essential systems have failed and his life expectancy, even if he does receive medical treatment, does not exceed two weeks.

The law regulates the medical treatment due to the terminally ill, while forging the proper balance between the value of the sanctity of life on the one hand, and the value of the autonomy of a person's wishes together with the importance of quality of life on the other.[6] Section 1 of the law makes clear that it is:

> "… based on the values of the State of Israel as a Jewish and democratic state, and on fundamental principles of ethics, morality and religion."[7]

The law further makes it very clear that:

> "Nothing in the law permits any action, even medical treatment, which is intended to kill, or will almost certainly cause the patient's death, whether or not such action is performed out of kindness and compassion, and whether or not the patient himself or another person requests it."[8]

Therefore active euthanasia and suicide remain strictly forbidden.

The novel feature of the law is a system which is a delayed-response timer which can turn the respirator off automatically at a pre-determined time. The timer would operate for 24 hours at a time and set off a red light or alarm after 12 hours as a reminder to reset it. The patient or his representative could at any time request an extension, but if the dying person were to insist, the timer would turn off the respirator at the end of the cycle. To date this has not been implemented anywhere else in the world. Indeed, Professor Avraham Steinberg has noted that since the idea of the timer became known abroad, many Gentile doctors have expressed interest in it, because medical teams of all views and backgrounds feel uncomfortable turning off a dying patient's respirator and causing his death.

Dr Y. M. Barilan observes that the concept of ventilators on timers is not new. Professor Meir, the director general of Shaare Tzedek, a religious hospital in Israel, proposed the concept of ventilators on timers to Rabbi Waldenberg as far back as 1976.[9] Rabbi Waldenberg endorsed the idea that year, some thirty years ago.[10] Additionally, in the 1990s Rabbi M. Shternbuch also endorsed, in certain circumstances, the use of ventilators on timers.[11] Dr Barilan writes that he cannot understand why this solution was not implemented sooner.[12]

Professor Vardit Ravitsky[13] raises the following issues concerning timers and also provides some theological background to the concept. She asks:

"What is the bioethical meaning of this proposed solution? If the reluctance to disconnect a patient from a ventilator is based on the belief that the act is ethically wrong, timers could be perceived as deceptive devices meant to disguise an unethical act as a legitimate one. In such a case, a mechanical device that transforms what is in essence withdrawal into what externally looks like withholding has controversial ethical implications. Do timers represent the 'displacement of ethics by trickery?' Will they enable Israeli physicians to perform in practice what their principles otherwise forbid them from doing, thus eroding a well founded ethical intuition and encouraging wrongdoing?"

She answers that "timers are not a ruse to an unethical outcome." This is because the termination of continuous treatment is prohibited by halachah, not because it leads to an ethically wrong outcome, but because:

"... it uses an ethically questionable procedure to achieve that outcome, as in the case of using tainted evidence to achieve a justified conviction. The difficulty of accepting withdrawal is not based on a belief that the life of a suffering dying patient should be prolonged at all costs but on a cultural approach that is ethically [halachically] opposed to human intervention to terminate life.

"Consequently, creating an alternative procedure allows the *halachic* legislator to overcome the obstacle and proceed towards achieving the desirable outcome. Finding an alternative procedure to a desirable outcome is a typical Halachic approach. It allows adaptation to changing circumstances without requiring the Halachic legislator to contradict legal principles or precedents."

Timers convert "commissions into omissions" and are thus intended to enable healthcare providers to overcome a procedural obstacle to achieve an ethically justified outcome. They may also allow them, writes Professor Ravitsky, to overcome a possible emotional difficulty of terminating life support treatment.

"Timers should therefore be perceived as an appropriate way of bridging the gap between the ethically justified outcomes of respect for individual autonomy, avoidance of prolonged suffering, and death with dignity, on the one hand, and communitarian values on the other."[14]

Amongst other things, this brief chapter verifies an important fact, namely, that when ministers of religion and doctors come together – in a framework of mutual respect and unity of purpose – they may find constructive ways to deal with issues that are within the realm of halachah and at the same time fully operational within a medical environment.

Notes

1. *Responsa Igrot Moshe* HM 2:75:1, see also *Responsa Teshuvot Vehanhagot*, (Jerusalem, 1992), 1:859.

2. Commentary *Ran, T. B. Nedarim* 40a, see also *T. B. Ketubot* 104a.

3. See A. Steinberg translated by Fred Rosner, *Encyclopedia of Jewish Medical Ethics* (Israel: Feldheim, 2003), volume 3, pp. 1057-62. See also earlier works, Chief Rabbi Ha'Rav Lord I. Jakobovits, *Jewish Medical Ethics* (Bloch: NY, 1975) p. 276 and F. Rosner and J. D. Bleich *Jewish Bioethics,* (NY: Hebrew Publishing Company, 1985), pp. 253-65.

4. It is important to note that where a situation exists where the doctor feels that treatment would save the life of a person but the person has requested that no treatment be administered, and should the doctor administer treatment he will be disciplined and struck off, he is within his halachic rights *not* to treat the patient. Halachah does not require him to lose his livelihood (*Shulchan Shlomoh,* volume 1, p. 136, and see *Nishmat Avraham,* volume 4, OH 656 p. 97).

5. *Jerusalem Post,* 12 November 2006

6. Prof. Avraham Steinberg, Israeli Ministry of Justice website, *Parshat HaShavua* column (Hebrew), edition no. 238, on the subject of *Terminally Ill Patients.*

7. *The Terminally Ill Patients' Law,* 2005 section 1.

8. *The Terminally Ill Patients' Law,* 2005 section 19.

9. Dr Barilan states that the year the question was asked was 1978, it was in fact two years earlier i.e. 1976 since the Hebrew date of Professor Meir's letter to Rav Waldenberg was 13th Sivan 5736 (1976) and the reply was written on 22nd Sivan, just ten days later.

10. *Responsa Tzitz Eliezer* (1985) 13:89.

11. *Responsa Teshuvot Vehanhagot,* 1:858 p.561.

12. Y. M. Barilan, *Is The Clock Ticking for Terminally Ill Patients in Israel? Preliminary Comment on a Proposal for a Bill of Rights for*

the Terminally Ill, J Med Ethics 2004, vol. 30, p. 356 and footnote ad loc.

13. A member of the Israeli Public Committee on the Dying Patient during 2000-2002.

14. Professor V. Ravitsky, *Timers on Ventilators,* BMJ, volume 330, 19 February 2005, pp. 416-417. For a fuller account of *The Terminally Ill Patients' Law,* 2005 and the halachic aspects appertaining to it see *Death With Dignity* by Simon M. Jackson, www.torahmitzion. org/eng/resources/JewishLaw.asp.

Glossary

Aron Ha'Kodesh – Holy Ark. This is found in the synagogue and contains the Torah Scrolls.

Beth Din – Rabbinic Court consisting of at least three judges called Dayanim (sing. Dayan).

Brachah – A blessing. This is recited over a wide range of things including food, a wonder of nature and before reading from the Torah.

Call-up/Synagogue honour – Men are called to recite a blessing when the Torah is read and this is considered a great honour. Other honours include raising the Torah Scroll for the audience to see, dressing the Torah Scroll and opening the Holy Ark.

Chessed – An act of kindness.

Cohen (pl. Cohanim) – A person descended from Aaron the first High Priest. The descendants functioned as priests in the Temple.

Duchan – The blessing given by the Cohanim to the people.

Haggadah – The book which is used at the Passover Seder ceremony relating the slavery in Ancient Egypt and subsequent Exodus.

Halachah (halachic) – Jewish Law.

Kiddush – Sanctification. A special blessing recited over wine on Shabbat and major festivals.

Minyan – A quorum of at least ten men required to enable the recitation of certain prayers.

Mishnah – A compilation of rabbinic teachings redacted by Rabbi Judah the Prince in the second century CE.

Mitzvah (pl. mitzvot) – A commandment in the Torah.

Responsum (pl. responsa) – A written halachic discourse from a rabbi to a person or community who asked a question.

Shabbat – The Sabbath which is observed on Saturdays.

Shulchan Aruch – A definitive guide to Jewish practice written by Rabbi Joseph Caro in the sixteenth century.

Talmud (Also called *Gemara*) – This expands the teachings of the Mishnah. It was written in the fifth century CE and contains complex rabbinic discussion spanning the earlier centuries. It remains to this day a source of halachic guidance.

Tephillin – Phylacteries. These are leather boxes worn on the bicep and head containing four hand-written paragraphs from the Torah that relate the Exodus from Egypt and belief in God.

Torah – The Five Books of Moses (Pentateuch) written by hand on parchment. Additionally, the term 'the Torah way of thinking' refers to the general way of thinking as found in the Pentateuch and rabbinic literature.

Yahrtzeit – The anniversary of the death of a loved one.

Yiddishkeit – Judaism in Yiddish.